A PAST and PRESENT Companion

The
Ffestiniog Railway
Past and Present

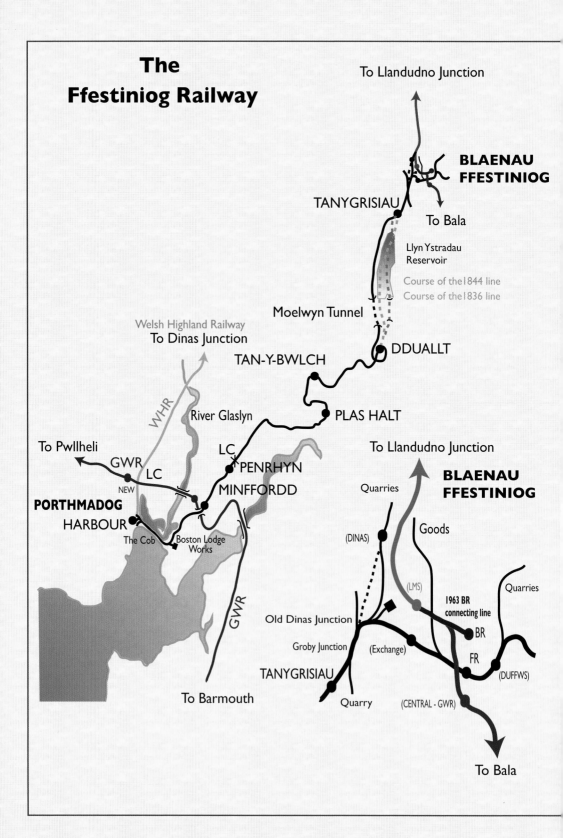

The Ffestiniog Railway

To Llandudno Junction

BLAENAU FFESTINIOG

TANYGRISIAU

To Bala

Llyn Ystradau Reservoir

Course of the 1844 line
Course of the 1836 line

Moelwyn Tunnel

DDUALLT

Welsh Highland Railway
To Dinas Junction

TAN-Y-BWLCH

WHR

River Glaslyn

PLAS HALT

To Llandudno Junction

BLAENAU FFESTINIOG

To Pwllheli

GWR

LC

LC

PENRHYN

NEW

MINFFORDD

Quarries

Goods

PORTHMADOG

(DINAS)

HARBOUR

The Cob

Boston Lodge Works

(LMS)

Quarries

1963 BR connecting line

BR

GWR

Old Dinas Junction

Groby Junction

(Exchange)

FR

(DUFFWS)

TANYGRISIAU

To Barmouth

Quarry

(CENTRAL - GWR)

To Bala

A PAST and PRESENT Companion

The
FFESTINIOG RAILWAY
Past and Present
John Stretton

150 YEARS OF STEAM POWER
1863
STEAM 150
2013
ON THE FFESTINIOG RAILWAY

Past and
Present

Past & Present Publishing Ltd

First published in 2013

British Library Cataloguing in Publication Data
A catalogue record for this book is available from the British Library.

ISBN 978 1 85895 282 6
Subscribers' Limited Edition 978 1 85895 283 3

Past & Present Publishing Ltd
The Trundle
Ringstead Road
Great Addington
Kettering
Northants NN14 4BW

Tel/Fax: 01536 330588
email: sales@nostalgiacollection.com
Website: www.nostalgiacollection.com

Printed and bound in the Czech Republic

Acknowledgements

As always, I am indebted to a wide variety and number of people who have assisted in one way or another. Photographers, especially, have been very willing to submit their images for consideration and I am truly grateful to those who aided in this way – without them and their foresight in pointing the camera at strategic moments the book would have struggled to be born! They are duly credited throughout the collection, but I take this opportunity to offer all of them my profound gratitude. In addition, there are those who have helped me before and have been fool enough to put their name in the frame again!

Amongst all of these, there are some who deserve especial mention and I would like to here present my sincere thanks to (in no particular order): Howard Wilson, Peter Arnold, Tony Baker, Mike Smith, Bryan Boskett, John Gilks, Cliff Thomas, and proof-readers Andy Savage, Adrian Gray and Allan Garraway. Finally, as usual, thanks go to all at Silver Link – Peter for encouragement and for putting up with countless phone calls, and David and Will for their unflinching patience and courtesy. Thank you all! The illustrations credited 'MJS' are mine.

Contents

Great things are often achieved by persons of vision, passion and enthusiasm. A 'can do' attitude overcomes obstacles, to arrive at what may have seemed impossible to the 'doubters'. Alan Pegler had all three attributes, as well as a determination not to be beaten, as was demonstrated throughout his life. Without him, we would not have had the Ffestiniog Railway that we all now enjoy and this book would (most likely) not have seen the light of day. It is, therefore, with very great pleasure and admiration that your author and your publisher proudly dedicate this volume to the man and his achievement in saving the FR in 1954. *John Morgan, MJS collection*

Throughout its 'new' life, since rescue in 1954, the railway has proved that progress came with fun, joy and spectacle, together with occasional hours of hard work and uncertainty! Galas have been a speciality over the past two decades, giving staff, volunteers and visiting public alike delightful and different menus and styles of operation. On May Day 1999 one of the railway's oldest locomotives, England engine No 4 *Palmerston*, is about to cross the weighbridge crossing on the approach to Minffordd station with the 0940 shuttle from Porthmadog, with *Bronllwyd* on other end. *MJS*

Introduction

As you will see, this volume is dedicated to the memory of Alan Pegler OBE FRSA, who died in March 2012 after a short illness. Without him we would not have had the railway as we know it now and we would all have been the poorer. His obituary has featured in many national publications and it is right that he should have been so honoured

I am pleased to be presenting this third volume of Past and Present books celebrating the Ffestiniog Railway, an organisation that has given countless hours of pleasure and satisfaction to many, many thousands of visitors and volunteers, as well as the staff who help to keep the show on the road. Much has happened over the years since Volumes 1 and 2 hit the bookstalls, in 1998 and 2005 – seemingly, as this is written and the book prepared in 2012, it is something of a seven-year itch! Over the last seven, the Welsh Highland Railway has progressed ever onwards towards Porthmadog and, from 2011, has run services over Britannia Bridge and into Harbour station. This has obviously impacted on the FR and led to work to widen the Cob, ready for a new platform to be constructed to serve both railways. This development is included herein to show,

once again, that the FR is not afraid of a challenge and that it will adapt to succeed.

I derive much pleasure from the production of these books, especially in the challenge of identifying precise locations, vantage points and even the length of lens used by past photographers. This is then heightened by the joy of visiting these locations to capture the present-day versions – sometimes even in the rain! There are various stages before completion of the project and all have their own delights, but preparing a third volume of a book is both easier and harder than the first outing! This latest is a mixture of both, but with the added pressure of the book being all-colour and the sourcing of past images of suitable quality and interest. There are b&w prints aplenty of the railway over the past 60 years, but colour shots are much scarcer, not least due to the cost of film and its quality way back then. Scanning those film images and converting to digital for the modern-day publishing processes has presented its own challenges, with all the scanning being done by myself. I am happy to say that the delights and satisfactions far outweigh whatever negatives there may be (and I am not talking photography here!) and I hope that you, the reader, will enjoy the results.

A common theme with previous offerings has been the cooperation and support from the railways concerned – as it should be of course – but I am pleased to say that the FR has been ever helpful. To all concerned I hereby tender my sincere thanks and gratitude – they have made the putting together of words and pictures a delight. As those who know me will be aware, I do not like re-using images previously included in publications, but in this collection I make no excuses for revisiting just one or two images – I hope readers will understand and forgive me!

Remember those black & white days, when life seemed so much more relaxed and peaceful and the sun always shone? Taking time out from volunteering labours in and around Harbour station are, left to right, Arthur Lambert, Alan Heywood and Alan Skellern, pausing to have their portraits captured for posterity at the station on 30 July 1961. Being a Sunday, the three have possibly just finished their morning duties, including carriage-oiling. *Mike Smith*

So, we celebrate 150 years of steam on the FR and, for this reason, there is a section dedicated to the locomotives, a handful of which have been around for the whole period! I have also included a few showing volunteers at work, as I feel that their behind-the-scenes work can be too often missed by the public and overlooked by the authorities.

I have derived great delight in 'going back in time', which is not always easy, with tree growth especially irksome at times, together with the difficulty of judging just where the original photographer was standing. Deep down I feel we all enjoy wallowing in nostalgia and I hope that you will equally enjoy this journey. The images have been carefully chosen and I hope you will

excuse the occasional diversion from a strict 'past and present' comparison; some of the images deserve to be seen for their own merit alone. We are fortunate that there were – and still are – skilful, dedicated and energetic photographers who thought nothing of travelling the length and breadth of the UK to capture images on film. There are undoubtedly more views of the railway 'out there' – and there have been too many left out of this volume purely through space. I would be delighted to hear of any, especially from those who have not had their work previously published. Finally, by all means use this book as a sort of travel, guide to go out and enjoy yourselves!

FROCS (Ffestiniog Railway Occasional Costume Society) is an unofficial element of the railway that adds to the public's enjoyment by 'dressing up', often in costumes that represent periods of the railway's past. On 16 October 1999 the next generation of Heywood – Kevin – is happy to proffer the time of day at Harbour station to a well-dressed potential traveller, played by another volunteer, Tammy Stretton. *Judi Stretton*

Seen from Garth Road in Porthmadog in October 1963, the narrowness of the spit of land on which the FR's southern terminus resides is plain to see, surrounded on all sides by water. Britannia Bridge stands to the left, and Britannia Terrace and Foundry in the centre, beyond the station, while the mile-long Cob runs off to the right. In the right distance, the mini-mountain of the quarry at Minffordd rises out of the autumn mist, with the real things barely visible in the distance. The harbour itself is very quiet.

Just short of five decades later the view, though obviously the same location, is dramatically changed. A greater number of regimented vessels populate the harbour, while on shore the FR station is surrounded by new developments and the old Foundry has been replaced by an anonymous and featureless Inland Revenue building. At 0955 on 12 June 2012 there is no mist and the distant mountains are far more obvious, but progressive excavation of the quarry has reduced its profile to below the horizon.

Norman Pearce, Howard Wilson collection/MJS

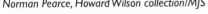

Down at ground level, the Harbour station building now stands proud of its neighbours in this view from March 1964. The headshunt track has been lifted in preparation for clearing the site for development of the wharf. There is an open feeling to the area, due not least to the road and station land only being separated by a small 'No Entry' sign. Note also the emptiness of the car park. The lorry looks like a Ford Thames Trader.

Moving ahead in time to 11 June 2012, the whole ambience has become one of control and tidiness. The now tarmacked road is graced with double yellow lines and the sharp bend has been smoothed by the addition of a spanning bridge over the corner of the harbour. The railway is securely bounded by a metal fence, the car park is full, the station building has been smartened, and there is a canopy over the platform.
Norman Pearce, Howard Wilson collection/MJS

Looking north from the end of the line, the focus in the foreground is the three-way turnout, a feature of operations in the early years of restoration. During a visit to the railway in 1955 the photographer again captures the openness so prevalent in those days, with the public able to wander carefree around the site. A lot of clearance has taken place but the track is yet to be de-weeded.

Forward to April 1964, and the work to alter the track layout has only recently been completed, as witnessed by the very clean ballast around the tracks. Note how the turnouts by the water tower have now been staggered. After removal the three-way point was taken first to Boston Lodge, to Glan y Mor yard, and thence after several years to Minffordd, where it still resides.

On another 36 years, and things are again being rethought. With ever-increasing traffic and demand for trains, the number and size of rolling stock also grew, leading to the need for more siding space within the Harbour station site. On 4 March 2000, before the season has begun, the redesign is in hand, which will result in there being six roads available. Note also that since 1964 the gap between the old station building and the goods shed has been infilled, creating what has become 'Spooner's' restaurant and bar, and a canopy has been installed.

John Wilkins, Bryan Boskett collection/ Norman Pearce, Howard Wilson collection/Tammy Stretton

Being the southern terminus, Harbour station provides facilities for locos to be coaled and watered. On 29 May 1970 the original *Earl of Merioneth* pauses for appropriate refreshment, with a healthy supply of coal alongside. Built in 1886 as *Livingston*

Thompson – renamed *Taliesin* in 1932, then *Earl of Merioneth* in 1963 – it was here nearing the end of its active career on the FR. After two decades in storage, almost derelict, it was cosmetically restored and sent to a new and better home at the National Railway Museum in York.

The provision for the locomotives here changed a number of times over the years, not least during the period when the fleet burned oil as opposed to coal, and the very latest arrangement is seen on 11 June 2012, as the new *Earl of Merioneth* – built by the railway 93 years after its predecessor, in 1979 – prepares to move off to run round its train, after arriving with the 1150 departure from Blaenau Ffestiniog. *Ray Ruffell, Silver Link collection/MJS*

In the 21st century it is hard to envisage how things were when those early youthful visionaries took on the task of renovation, and just what a mammoth job the railway presented to them. This view from 10 July 1953, two years after the first suggestions of a Society and its ambitions, and one year before Alan Pegler acquired the railway, the derelict state at Harbour station is there for all to see. Literally abandoned after the cessation of operations in 1946, nature is taking hold but, quite incredibly, there is no sign of any vandalism over the succeeding seven years.

A little under five years later the transformation is impressive. On 26 May 1958 double-Fairlie *Taliesin* (ex-*Livingston Thompson*, later *Earl of Merioneth*) stands in Harbour station waiting to form a train to Tan y Bwlch, which had been reopened by the restorationists just the previous month. Roughly halfway to the ultimate goal of Blaenau Ffestiniog, reaching that location was no mean feat, with the railway climbing more than 400 feet above Harbour in less than 7½ miles. Note the neat and tidy platform, signage and station building. *T. C. Cole collection, MJS collection/Gerald Adams, MJS collection*

In the first view, from 1955, the station area has been cleared of the abandoned rolling stock and initial passenger services have begun. Here a visitor takes the opportunity of chatting to the crew of *Prince* before the short run across the Cob to Boston Lodge. The weeds are still growing but at least there is life back in the station.

In the first two decades of the railway's resurgence there were relatively few photographs of the line in winter ... and even fewer services! In a rare snow view at Harbour in early 1970, the scene looks decidedly cold as a rake of 'Centenary'-style 'Barn' coaches waits to form an infrequent winter service. Note the old Tannoy horn on the station wall and Richard Herington, of the Midland Group working party, returning to work redecorating the ladies' toilet.

Another example of the railway enjoying itself! On a bright and sunny 30 April 2000, '*Thomas* and friends' have invaded the railway for the weekend, with, left to right, *Duke* (ex-*Palmerston*), *Prince* and *Earl* with their smiley faces entertaining the visitors. Note the emergence of the white-fronted gift shop and 'Spooner's' eatery.

John Wilkins, Bryan Boskett collection/Howard Wilson/ Tammy Stretton

The station throat, heading to the Cob embankment, has seen many changes over the past five decades, but this October 1958 view of *Prince*, shunting a rake of permanent way wagons, is little changed from the days of the original company. In the background a short rake of slate wagons is on the still extant rails outside the old goods shed, while to the right Britannia Foundry is still operational.

Track changes have accompanied the ever-increasing traffic needs, not least in making for easier negotiation of the sidings in Harbour station. Comparison with the earlier view shows greater utilisation of the seaward land to the left of the main running line, together with the disappearance of the Foundry building on the right, replaced by Inland Revenue offices. Over the weekend of 22/23 August 2009 services on the FR were double-headed and loaded to 10 or 11 coaches. On the Saturday, 22 August, *Prince* heads *Blanche* away from Harbour, making a spirited exit with the 10-coach 1015 departure for Blaenau Ffestiniog. *Palmerston* and *Taliesin* handled alternate trains. *Mike Esau/MJS*

Built between 1807 and 1811 by William Madocks MP, the mile-long Cob embankment, blocking the Afon Glaslyn's route to the sea, served to eventually provide access to Porthmadog by both road and rail, in addition to its land reclamation function in conjunction with sluice gates at Britannia Bridge. The magnitude of the undertaking across the tidal estuary can be glimpsed from this view from October 1983, looking towards Boston Lodge at the other end, as *Mountaineer* accelerates away from Harbour station.

Undoubtedly the greatest structural change since the Cob's construction has been brought about by the arrival of the rebuilt Welsh Highland Railway at Harbour station from 2011. The need to accommodate trains of both railways at the same time has led to the project to widen the Cob at the station throat, which will eventually see a platform serving both lines. This view from one of the railway's offices on 12 March 2012 shows the final days of the major work of dropping stones into the estuary and forming a new base for the future FR running lines.

The FR is excellent at remembering and recreating its past. As an example, (*inset below*) this train, made up of four vintage carriages and with authentic loco and appropriately dressed fireman, could almost have been from a century earlier. On 16 October 2005, 1879-vintage *Merddin Emrys* nears the end of its journey with the 1200 service from Blaenau Ffestiniog, as it crosses the Cob and enters Harbour station throat. The railway is, indeed, blessed by having so much of its motive power, stock and infrastructure intact from the late-Victorian era. *John Morgan, MJS collection/MJS (2)*

Part way across the Cob and looking back towards Porthmadog, it is clear how snugly the town sits under the shadow of Moel-y-Gest. Without William Madocks's vision, the town of Portmadoc, named after him, would not have been created or developed in the way that it has. This view from Easter 1952 shows the moribund railway and station complex, the sea at low tide and the wharf, on the left, abandoned. All is very quiet and, with much of the town's income stream removed, it was truly a case of 'perchance it is not dead, but merely sleepeth'!

The modern view from a similar point on 12 March 2012 shows not only the vitality and presence that has blossomed since the earlier view, but also the work in widening the Cob at this end and the preparations for the new platform, with the FR lines to go to the seaward side. Stone had been laid and flattened, ready as a base for ballasting, following the creation of the wave wall to the left of the rails. *David Morgan/MJS*

We now move further away from Porthmadog, during what is thought to be the FRS AGM on 30 March 1957, to view *Taliesin*, in grey undercoat, accelerating across the Cob en route to a newly restored Penrhyn station, which was formally opened to the public on 20 April. The loco looks in good condition and the Cob itself has obviously received a certain amount of TLC over the past couple of years. Note the telegraph wires on the seaward side, which had survived in remarkably good shape considering the years of inattention.

Fifty-five years later, it is clear that much time and effort has been expended in making the place as presentable and operationally efficient as possible. With a storm gathering behind, the 'new' *Earl of Merioneth* accelerates across the Cob on Sunday 6 May 2012 during the FR 'Blaenau 30' Gala, at the head of the 1015 service for Blaenau Ffestiniog, and proudly wearing one of the original 1982 headboards. 'Order, Order' was often heard from the then Speaker of the House of Commons, George Thomas, who was a great supporter of the railway; his signature graces the headboard. The overhead telegraph wires were replaced by ground-level cables during the early 1960s. *John Wilkins, Bryan Boskett collection/MJS*

Going back in time and further across the Cob, the condition of the embankment at Easter 1952 is showing signs of attack by inclement weather since abandonment in 1946. With sand being blown onto the track from gales and/or strong winds, as well as the growth of turf, etc, the idea that the railway could be reborn is probably not at the forefront of the photographer's mind!

Once again the staff and volunteers have wrought marvels over the years, with this view from 11 June 2012 evidencing the appreciation of both aesthetics and operational requisites. The footpath to the right is now much more likely to protect the public from falling to the road below. *David Morgan/MJS*

The first 'station' on the restored railway was Pen Cob Halt, at the end of the Cob and immediately before the entrance to Boston Lodge Works. Opening with Boston Lodge Halt in 1955, it only lasted as an 'active' stop for a short period; having been very little used over the years, it was formally closed in 1968. As can be seen from this view of *Linda* approaching in September 1966, there is nothing other than the nameboard to indicate its presence.

An undated view from around 1964 sees *Linda* again passing the site, roughly marked by the lower-quadrant point indicator alongside the second coach. The turnout under this carriage leads into the Boston Lodge Works yard. The fireman is taking it easy before the climb and the hard work begins. Once again Moel-y-Gest dominates the skyline on the left, with the equivalent rising behind Tremadog to the right. *John Gilks/Norman Pearce, Howard Wilson collection*

Situated on a near 90-degree bend on the A487 at the end of the Cob, Boston Lodge Works began as a quarry providing stone for the construction of the embankment, and a workshop to service the tramway waggons used to transport it and their horses. The facility became the maintenance yard for the Cob, and when the railway was begun in 1832 it was taken over as the wagon works and smithy for that enterprise. This

makes it the world's oldest working railway workshops in continuous use, apart from the interregnum period between 1947 and 1954. The name Boston Lodge refers to William Madocks's Parliamentary constituency in Lincolnshire and was applied to the prominent cottages, originally barracks and offices for the Cob works and later, as now, accommodation for FR staff. Development and diversification began from the earliest days and has continued through to the 21st century, including the building of several locomotives for the railway. This undated view, probably from the early 1960s, shows staff accommodation to the left and the fortress-like entrance to the yard.

Operational dictates over the years have brought many changes, not least in the yard itself and the entrance thereto. On 6 May 2012, in a view slightly further out onto the Cob, the fortress walls have gone, as have some buildings in the yard and the chimney from the boiler house. Note that, in these days of Health & Safety, the public footpath is protected at this end and access to the yard denied. *Norman Pearce, Howard Wilson collection/MJS*

Seen behind the Works in the photographs opposite, the rock wall created by the early quarrying rises above and dominates the yard. On 27 March 1983 the view from 'on high' shows the relatively new carriage shed to the left and the more ancient, later demolished, 'Long Shed' to the right, with the 1979-vintage *Earl of Merioneth* between, resting between duties. The fortress gates and pillars have gone by this date.

With the growth of both trees and bushes over the ensuing years, the precise vantage point is now only accessible by seriously risking one's safety, hence the view on 11 June 2012 is from a point slightly to the right. Yet more of the old stone wall by the running line has gone, as has the 'Long Shed', its position marked by the pit, left of centre, in the yard. At 1035 on this morning, *Vale of Ffestiniog* stands in the yard, alongside NGG16 Garratt No 87, which is about to depart for Harbour and a run to Caernarfon on the Welsh Highland Railway. The area in the centre of the view, outside the Erecting Shop, was concreted for hard standing during the 2012 Kids' Training Week.
John Morgan/MJS

Back at ground level, the Works complex is seen in 1961, after seven years of occupancy by the new FR, with the area and buildings in much the same state and condition as inherited, apart from the clearance of a 'jungle'. *Moelwyn* stands on one of two entrances to the main workshop, while 'Bug Boxes' stand on the other line into the works. *Merddin Emrys*'s

original cab, sadly never to be used again, rests on a wagon on the left. The closeness and scale of the escarpment behind can clearly be seen.

Again from a slightly wider viewpoint, the buildings have seen both renovation and some alteration, with the tall chimney the immediate absentee, in a view that is both smarter and tidier. At 1108 on 11 June 2012, *Vale of Ffestiniog* waits to be called across the Cob for duty. The pit in the foreground lies where the previously mentioned 'Long Shed' once stood. *Norman Pearce, Howard Wilson collection/MJS*

While concentration in the early days was naturally on using whatever was to hand that was serviceable, items not immediately required or available found storage. Much came to be temporarily 'dumped' in Glan y Mor yard, on the southern edge of the Works complex; in this undated view around May 1965, *Palmerston*, painted pink, presents a forlorn spectacle – hardly one that inspires confidence of restoration to running order! Condemned at this point, the loco was sold to a group of individuals from Derby Research (BR) and, fortunately for us all today, was retrieved! The shed frame is being erected in the background, on this side of the Works complex.

With the passing of the years and the continual growth in passenger numbers and carriages to meet that demand, Glan y Mor land became more and more needed. Thus by 11 June 2012 the scene is hardly recognisable. A new carriage shed stands to the left, with a paint shop beyond, and redesigns at this end of the original Works in the middle distance. Coach No 123, a 2010/11 rebuild from 1970 Observation Car No 101, stands at the end of a rake between duties, while on the right a variety of freight stock is similarly between rosters. *Norman Pearce, Howard Wilson collection/MJS*

Let the train take the strain! In an undated view from around 1964, in green-and-white days, *Linda* sweeps around Boston Lodge curve, past the Works yard, with a train from Harbour station bound for Tan y Bwlch, at a speed much greater than the queue of cars held up by the Tollgate. The presence of queues at this end of the Cob was long a source of irritation for the motorist, due to the requirement of paying a small fee to cross the Cob, but here presents an interesting aside for the car-spotter! To the left of the loco are the remains of the wall that bounded the top end of the main yard at Boston Lodge, separating the railway's property from the Cob, which belonged to the Tremadoc Estate.

Running in the reverse direction, *Lyd* heads for its destination at Harbour on a bright 6 May 2012, with the 0850 roster from Blaenau Ffestiniog. Note that the passage of 58 years has seen fresh fencing on the boundary of the Works yard. Note also the clear road, due to the disappearance of the Toll and the opening of the Porthmadog bypass, and the provision of a footpath for walkers and cyclists to travel over the Cob to Porthmadog. It is pleasing to see the same style of carriages still in use. *Norman Pearce, Howard Wilson collection/MJS*

Those who have come to know the Ffestiniog over more recent years will not be aware of the many changes wrought at Boston Lodge since 1954. Perhaps one of the lesser-known is the former presence of massive gates astride the running line at the north end of the curve off the Cob, marking the end of the Tremadoc Estate and the point where the main line passed on to the company's own property. This view from 30 July 1961, looking south, reinforces the feeling of a fortress, with substantial wooden gates and massive stone pillars; the latter were removed after a fireman hit his head on one of them. Note that the boundary wall mentioned on page 26 is still in situ.

Apart from the main running line, albeit augmented with turnouts, the only remaining structure from the earlier view is the three stone slabs on the right, from the base of the old pillar, at the head of the stone steps leading down to the roadway. Although there is still a fence between the main line and the Works yard, the vista now has a much more open feel. The latterly little-used set of points at the head of the Tollgate Steps, taking a left curve into the Works yard in this view, were removed during the summer of 2012 by the permanent way gang, recovering some old bullhead track in the process. *Mike Smith/MJS*

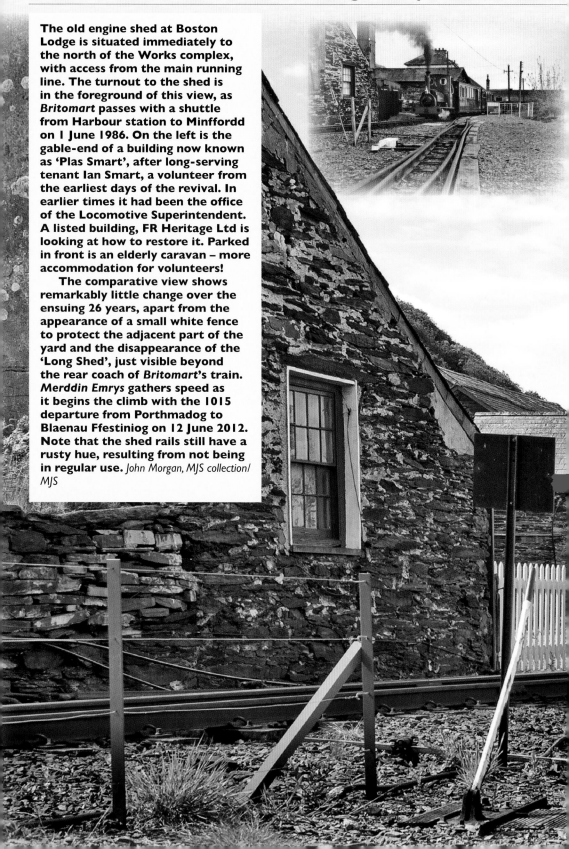

The old engine shed at Boston Lodge is situated immediately to the north of the Works complex, with access from the main running line. The turnout to the shed is in the foreground of this view, as *Britomart* passes with a shuttle from Harbour station to Minffordd on 1 June 1986. On the left is the gable-end of a building now known as 'Plas Smart', after long-serving tenant Ian Smart, a volunteer from the earliest days of the revival. In earlier times it had been the office of the Locomotive Superintendent. A listed building, FR Heritage Ltd is looking at how to restore it. Parked in front is an elderly caravan – more accommodation for volunteers!

The comparative view shows remarkably little change over the ensuing 26 years, apart from the appearance of a small white fence to protect the adjacent part of the yard and the disappearance of the 'Long Shed', just visible beyond the rear coach of *Britomart*'s train. *Merddin Emrys* gathers speed as it begins the climb with the 1015 departure from Porthmadog to Blaenau Ffestiniog on 12 June 2012. Note that the shed rails still have a rusty hue, resulting from not being in regular use. *John Morgan, MJS collection/ MJS*

Following the introduction of steam locomotion in place of horses in 1863, a few years later the aforementioned two-road stone engine shed was built alongside the running line. In 1879 a second shed was constructed in corrugated metal on the valley side, and each had tall chimney flues to take away engine smoke. In this undated view from around 1970 the original is to the right, with track to the 'newer' (but more dilapidated) addition now removed and the pit filled in. Note that the metal shed had been shortened in the 1940s following storm damage. All seems to have suffered from the exigencies of wind and weather in this exposed spot.

The shortened corrugated-iron edifice was later removed, replaced by a breeze-block construction that was itself demolished and replaced by the new addition seen here, built to the full 1887 length at this end. The growth of trees over the years to 12 June 2012 now hides the view of the distant mountains. *Norman Pearce, Howard Wilson collection/MJS*

At the top end of the engine shed was a curiously shaped, trapezoidal, building that housed weighing machines for slate wagons passing to the right on a former alignment of the main line between about 1850 and 1872. This forms the background to a busy scene at Boston Lodge Halt in 1955, as *Prince* reaches the temporary terminus shortly after the reopening on 23 July. The driver casually leans on the cab as his passengers, young and old, leave the train for a brief stroll.

↘ By 11 June 2012 the scene is very much tidier, with some renovations to the old weigh house, gardening and replacement fencing alongside the line, and a distinct platform edge to serve the travelling public. On this occasion, however, there are no passengers requesting a stop and *Earl of Merioneth* steams straight through with the 1015 service from Porthmadog to Blaenau Ffestiniog. *John Wilkins, Bryan Boskett collection/MJS*

On the approach to Minffordd station the track appears to be double, but the second line is actually a long siding that also leads to the steep gradient down to the once active exchange sidings with the ex-British Rail 'Cambrian Coast' route. To accurately account for the goods being transhipped between standard and narrow gauge, weighing facilities were installed alongside the main running line, complete with a weigh house. The latter is seen in June 1971 as a northbound train enters the station (out of sight).

Four decades later, the weigh house still stands, though no longer in use for its original purpose. Its small outhouse has lost its roof and now has a castellated topping, and the previous boundary wall to the left has gone, replaced by a slate and stone platform, here bearing spare rails. The scene on 12 June 2012 looks decidedly smarter than of yore. *Norman Pearce, Howard Wilson collection/MJS*

Moving to the other side of the weigh house and looking back in 1962, the two weighing tables can be seen between the tracks. The window facing these machines has been boarded up and the weigh house, its surroundings and the track all look in need of attention. In the distance *Mary Ann* and *Moelwyn* make their way towards the turnout for the run down into the lower yard, while the long siding beyond contains empty slate wagons.

By 3 May 1993, during one of the famous FR Galas, attention has most certainly been lavished on the scene, both on the weigh house, with its restored window and, most noticeably, on the track, which now would stand any inspection. A most unusual sight on this day is the use of a Pilotman (standing at the front of the running plate) as a sort of 'human token' to facilitate shuttle trips between the lower yard and Minffordd station, top-and-tailed by *Lilla* and the almost invisible *Britomart* at the far end. *Norman Pearce, Howard Wilson collection/MJS*

One of the major achievements over the years by the FR is to successfully encourage and cater for young volunteers. So many movements suffer from lack of interest from the younger generation but, by providing comfortable accommodation as well as interesting tasks, the Ffestiniog is ahead of the curve. A truly remarkable creation has been the hostel purpose-built by the railway and volunteers themselves at Minffordd. On 21 February 1995 the basic shape is plain to see, surrounded by scaffolding, but there is still much to do.

Just ten months later real progress has been made and work has not stopped for the inclement weather, revealed by the boot prints in the snow on 23 December 1995.

And so to 12 June 2012, and not only does the hostel still look highly attractive and well cared for, but it also fits superbly within its surroundings. With imaginative and thoughtful design, including the use of slate, it is a real credit to both the railway and those who helped to build it. *Tammy Stretton (2)/MJS*

The identity of the Double-Fairlie that saw the light of day as *Livingston Thompson* in 1886 has been convoluted, with various changes of name over its lifetime. Sometime known as *Taliesin*, then *Earl of Merioneth*, it is here seen in the former guise on 30 March 1957, in undercoat grey, as it heads south from Minffordd with a train from Penrhyn to Porthmadog during the FRS AGM day. This is self-evidently a special event, judging by the lineside photographers, the crowds just visible on Minffordd platform in the background and the film crew on the trackside.

The crowds are out in force again on 3 May 1993, but this time the event is broadcast by the yellow 'Steam Festival' notice to the left. One of the visiting locomotives for this May Day Bank Holiday weekend, *Velinheli*, an 1886-vintage Hunslet once extensively used at Dinorwic Quarry, heads a shuttle bound for Porthmadog, top-and-tailed with *Sgt Murphy*. Note the appearance of the electricity pylon. *John Wilkins, Bryan Boskett collection/MJS*

The FR has many unique features to attract the visitor, but the gravity slate train is one of the most unusual. Enabled by the ruling gradient being downhill from Blaenau Ffestiniog, created by the original railway to cater for bringing both slate and horses down to Harbour, the sight of a string

of slate waggons speeding south without external motive power always delights. On 1 May 1999 the train prepares to run down into the lower yard at Minffordd, with the first six waggons of this moderate-length rake holding brakemen with a warning horn.

A variation on the theme, and not one set up to entertain the public, is this gravity works train rumbling into Minffordd station on 6 May 2012, again bound for the lower yard, with the wagons now having somewhat more sophisticated braking systems and the inhabitants not forced to endure the discomfort of riding on slate edging! Note the presence of hi-vis vests, now de rigueur for railway line working, and the new bridge in the distance, taking the railway over the bypass. *John Morgan, MJS collection/MJS*

The engines go in two by two! A most unusual but highly delightful sight at Minffordd on 8 December 1973 sees BR Type 2 diesels Nos 5054 and 5076 pausing at Minffordd main-line station with the Wirral Railway Circle's 1L03 11-coach 'Cambrian Coast Express' from Crewe to Pwllheli and return. In the background *Linda* and *Blanche*, by now both oil-fired, approach Minffordd with their train from Porthmadog, unusually double-headed, to take some of the participants of the rail tour for a ride on the FR.
Norman Kneale, *MJS Collection*

Arriving at Minffordd station, and looking back towards Porthmadog, we see the new *Earl of Merioneth*, completed in 1979 at Boston Lodge, approaching with the 'Mountain Prince', a non-stop Porthmadog-Blaenau Ffestiniog morning train in August 1987. Begun in that year, this daily service was an attempt to entice passengers onto the morning departure from Harbour, but it was not to last long. The interconnectivity of modes of transport at this location is highlighted by the bus and BR rail signs.

In the comparative view, the BR sign still points the way to the main-line station on 13 June 2012, 18 years into rail privatisation and now a 'National Rail' symbol. Its bus equivalent, however, has changed colour and design and lists far more services than previously. The road is still quiet, due to the opening of the bypass, as *Merddin Emrys* brings the 1015 Porthmadog-Blaenau Ffestiniog service up the gradient on a decidedly wet June day. There has been some clearance of bushes on the right. *John Gilks/MJS*

Machines do not always perform faultlessly, and on a decidedly dull day in April 1961 *Merddin Emrys* pauses for some attention, with concerned faces, a superfluity of steam, and *Mary Ann* in the background as backup. Without vacuum brakes on its first run out, with new tanks and leaking steam in the cold weather, it is certainly the centre of attention. Note the cars parked for the spectators, and the old traditional station sign, in BR(WR) colours of brown and cream.

Standing slightly further back, on the platform, the same vista sees *Prince* and *Blanche*, in rainy conditions, entering the station on 23 August 2009 with the first train of the day, the 1015 Porthmadog-Blaenau Ffestiniog. The main-line station sign is now of the double-arrow variety, colour light signals share space with a replica vintage FR circular signal, and the permanent way looks in fine shape.

John Wilkins, Bryan Boskett collection/MJS

The normal mode of FR operations is for trains to 'drive on the right', but this has not always been the case. Before the installation of auto-loops, all trains ran into the up platform in both directions unless the signalling was switched in. In this view from October 1965 *Prince*, with Bill Hoole driving, pauses with a down train, while *Linda*, going up, has carriages Nos 11 and 12 and Wickham trolley No 1543 in tow with a special works train. Earnest discussions between those on the ground and the engine crew do not seem to be merely routine, with Ron Lester, in trademark cap and pipe, approaching and passing a young Fred Howes. Note that on this side of the station there is a seat for waiting passengers but no platform, the boarding to cross between platforms is very narrow, and there is the large lever controlling the point in the foreground.

In the 21st century the scene is dramatically improved, with much attention given over the years to aesthetics, customer comfort and facilities, and health and safety. On 13 June 2012 *Earl of Merioneth* slows for the Minffordd stop with the 1340 Blaenau Ffestiniog-Porthmadog service, passing the superb replica of the original waiting shelter on this platform. *Norman Pearce, Howard Wilson collection/MJS*

From 1954 until the early 1980s the FR loco fleet wore a uniform green-panelled, red-lined livery, with the sole exception of the privately owned, light blue, *Britomart*. Since the 1980s the locomotives have worn different-coloured liveries, each having its own persona and usually settled into a regular colour. On 15 July 2000 *David Lloyd George* shows off its particular shade of red as it draws to a halt with the 1155 Blaenau Ffestiniog-Porthmadog working. With bright sunshine aiding in bringing out the best in colours generally, the red and cream of the carriages both complement the locomotive and add sparkle to the vision. With safety netting to the left, work is under way on a dry-stone wall behind the far platform, to create space for a waiting shelter.

The same vantage point shows off *Merddin Emrys*'s own individual coat, on 2 April 2011, compared with *David Lloyd George* behind, at the head of 'The Snowdonian' rail tour. For special invited and fare-paying guests, this was a celebration of the opening of the Welsh Highland Railway, travelling Porthmadog-Blaenau Ffestiniog-Caernarfon-Porthmadog. *Both MJS*

The carriages also had their own special window cards for the day. *MJS*

THE
SNOWDONIAN

PORTHMADOG
BLAENAU FFESTINIOG
CAERNARFON
PORTHMADOG

While not a regular sight for the general public, works trains are a necessary and vital tradition. The duties are usually allocated to the more mundane locomotives, often lower-powered to perform the less arduous rosters and of a type that do not mind the occasional 'war wounds' from the nature of the works undertaken. On 15 March 2009 *Moelwyn* rests briefly at Minffordd between duties at 1320 – lunchtime. At the rear is a new acquisition for

the railway, a crane purpose-fitted onto a low-loader to give maximum strength and capability for the task to be asked of it and easing the burden on the staff working the train. *Judi Stretton*

An innovation by the FR, which sadly did not seem to catch the public imagination, was 'Y Tren Siarad'/'The Talking Train'. With a view to enhancing visitor experience, various locations were designated – and marked with numbered plaques (see inset) – and pertinent histories/stories of those locations were to be had by pressing the relevant number on a handset given to the travellers for that purpose. On 9 April 2004 *Prince* stands in Minffordd station while participants explore the points located here. *Both MJS*

Often a money-spinner for preserved/private railways, charters are where a group of enthusiasts, usually photographers, are given privileged access to the railway to capture scenes that may not normally be available. On 31 May 1986 such a group is at Minffordd to record *Blanche* making a storming exit from the station with a train bound for Blaenau Ffestiniog. With regulation hi-vis vests on display, the tour members are able to choose some vantage points not normally used.

Since the construction and opening of the Porthmadog bypass, the same vantage point has disappeared, leading to this near-comparative view being taken from the approach road to Bron Turnor. About to cross the bright red bridge over the new road, *Merddin Emrys* accelerates away from Minffordd with the 1015 Porthmadog-Blaenau Ffestiniog duty on 12 June 2012. *John Morgan, MJS collection/MJS*

Although not a vantage point that received a lot of photographic exposure, this is nevertheless one that provided an attractive angle on down trains, close to the crossing giving access to 'Bron Turnor', the house in the background seen here on 30 March 1957. *Taliesin* is again seen in grey undercoat, coasting down the incline on the approach to Minffordd station with the AGM train from Penrhyn.

Once again the precise location has been removed by the arrival of Porthmadog's bypass. The house is still there but now hidden behind the trees on the far side of the railway, in this view during the early afternoon of 25 June 2012. *John Wilkins, Bryan Boskett collection/Neil Clayton*

Continuing the climb between Minffordd and Penrhyn, *Linda* puts in some effort as she gathers speed up Gwyndy Bank – albeit with empty coaching stock bound for Tan y Bwlch – passing the Clayton household and watched by visiting Judi Stretton on 2 May 2004. The diminutive headboard atop the smokebox exhorts one and all to 'See us at Railfest', the exhibition to be held at the NRM, York.

Slightly further up the line *Linda* is seen again, this time on 7 August 1967, passing Capel Nazareth with a train bound for Tan y Bwlch. The fireman leans from the cab of the 4.35pm departure from Porthmadog, to ensure that there are no obstacles as the service begins the approach to Penrhyn station. *MJS/Peter Arnold*

Taliesin in grey is the centre of attention once more on 30 March 1957, as it stands in Penrhyn station having run round its FRS AGM train before returning with it to Porthmadog. Operations were watched by a local resident on the extreme left, who was presumably intrigued to see a passenger train here, as the newly restored station will not formally open for another few weeks.

Fourteen years later the loop at Penrhyn is put to good use as *Linda* arrives with an up train on 21 July 1971, passing sister *Blanche* going in the opposite direction. The signalman is collecting the token from the up train, and will process it through the staff machine in the former goods shed before giving it, and permission to proceed, to the down train. This will then leave and allow passengers for or from the up train access to the platform. The up train will then receive its token and depart.

As the railway forged its way northwards over the years, the loop at Penrhyn fell out of use; last used in 1975, its removal came at the close of 1981. On 12 June 2012 the present layout is in view as *Earl of Merioneth* draws to a halt with the 1340 Blaenau Ffestiniog-Porthmadog roster, picking up just two passengers on this day. Note how spick and span everywhere looks and that the yard is graced with a token, disconnected siding, complete with a wagon turntable replicating its former provision to serve the goods shed. *John Wilkins, Bryan Boskett collection/Peter Arnold/MJS*

The view to the north of Penrhyn's station building, now converted for use as a
volunteer hostel, shows the creation of a smart-looking platform following the loop's
removal. On 7 October 2000 *Linda* is again the hard-worked motive power, heading
'Y Cymro', the 1500 from Porthmadog during the FR's Vintage Weekend. Note how
tight is the line to the right-hand wall, not helped by the greenery trying to spread
outwards!

   The comparative shot shows very little change, apart that the foliage on the wall
has been checked, giving a slightly clearer aspect for the houses beyond. On 12 June
2012 *Merddin Emrys* slows for a station stop while operating the 1335 Porthmadog-
Blaenau Ffestiniog service. *Tammy Stretton/MJS*

A 4085

John Townsend

Holiday Cottage w/

FFESTINIOG RLY GY L7

ENRHYDEUDRAETH

nel ANDREW MORRIS

1 UPTON GDNS, UPTON

N SEVERN WR8 ONN

1684/593510

As the railway leaves the station, to continue its journey north-eastwards, it crosses the A4085 road to Llanfrothen. Gates are closed to road traffic to allow the passage of trains, and these are manned at all times of railway operations. In July 1963 friendly crossing lady Ann Davies waves as *Merddin Emrys*, without cab roof, emerges from behind the wall with a down train from Tan y Bwlch. Note how open was the land surrounding the railway at this time.

At the same place today there is a decidedly different feel, and not just because of the wet road! Years of unchecked growth have clouded the hillside behind the train and blocked the previous view over the wall to the railway. *Earl of Merioneth* is allowed a little further out onto the road, therefore, for the present portrait, on a damp 11 June 2012, with the 1510 Blaenau Ffestiniog-Porthmadog turn. Hi-vis vests are the order of day now and the gate guardian is suitably garbed but hidden behind the train. *Norman Pearce, Howard Wilson collection/MJS*

Although the A4085 can be a busy road, the railway is happily not too much of a hindrance, as services are relatively few at normal times. The passage up the line across the road is relatively sedate and, in this undated view from 1965, *Linda* takes her time as she leaves Penrhyn, helping the aura of a hot and lazy summer's afternoon.

Over the weekend of 22/23 August 2009, services on the FR were double-headed and loaded to 10 or 11 coaches. On the Saturday, 22 August, *Prince* heads *Blanche* away from the Penrhyn station stop and over the road crossing with the 1015 Porthmadog-Blaenau Ffestiniog train. Note how the scene is now far more colourful, and not just because of the earlier view being in black & white. Not only has there been abundant verdant growth over the past four decades, but the buildings have also been tarted up, with bushes and flowers now proliferating in their gardens, while even the locos and trains have a variety of coats. *MJS collection/MJS*

With the ever-increasing traffic, it became more difficult to satisfy demand and run more and longer trains. A solution was to install extra loops to accommodate passing trains, and one was put in place at Rhiw Goch in November 1973. Three years prior to this, in July 1970, *Mountaineer* steadfastly pushes onwards and upwards with a train bound for Dduallt. With the railway often skirting around hilly outcrops, there were some magnificent views for the enjoyment of the travelling public. Note the WHR carriage in a short-lived varnished brown livery.

In the heart of the loop a down train waits patiently for Single-Fairlie *Taliesin* to cross. Fireman Matthew Cable takes time to exchange pleasantries with the crew of the down train in the late afternoon of 16 October 2005, as his charge makes its way towards **Tan y Bwlch.** *John Gilks/MJS*

One of the most dramatic structures on the whole railway, whether seen from the lineside or from the train, is the 62-foot-high dry-stone embankment known as Cei Mawr. Still largely as built, it obviously needs inspection and, where necessary, maintenance. For example, the parapet on the far side of this view was reconstructed in 1964. On 9 August 1969 *Blanche* hauls her six-coach train over the structure, with the drop to the east plainly visible.

A rare view on top of the embankment, with a forest of fir trees as backdrop, sees *Prince* working hard on 26 March 1983 on a runpast for members of an enthusiasts' photographic charter.
Peter Arnold/John Morgan, MJS collection

Plas Tan y Bwlch, a mansion that was once the home of William Oakley, quarry-owner, sits high up the hillside on the opposite side of the valley from Maentwrog. Sold out of private ownership for development in 1962, it was subsequently acquired by Gwynedd County Council for use as a conference and educational centre. With a view to possibly attracting traffic from below, on 1 June 1963 the FR opened Plas Halt alongside the line high above the house, with a pathway created to join the two. On 14 August 1992 *Merddin Emrys* passes the Halt in dappled sunshine on its way back down to Porthmadog.

At the opposite end of the Halt, the photographer is now level with the track to record *Prince* pausing to allow passengers to alight. A path down the steep escarpment on the left leads to the house. There are many walks through this woodland and the railway can be seen at close range at several points. *Both John Morgan, MJS collection*

From Plas Halt to Tan y Bwlch, a distance of a little over a mile, the line twists and turns through the woods in a distorted horseshoe. Roughly midway along this stretch the railway passes milepost 7, denoting the distance that has been travelled from Porthmadog. In October 1967 the original *Earl of Merioneth* skirts round the bend at this point and is about to enjoy the downward gradient of 1 in 80. The sharpness of the bends leads to up trains sounding as though they are about to enter Tan y Bwlch station, when in truth they are still about half a mile away! *John Gilks*

The up gradient through Tan y Bwlch station is 'only' 1 in 132, and no doubt *Merddin Emrys* is mightily relieved to have arrived on 22 April 1961 with the AGM train, on test and accompanied by the original *Earl of Merioneth*, but here with the nameplate as *Taliesin*. The amount of steam being produced and the obvious exertions are a fascination to the young spectators! *John Wilkins, Bryan Boskett collection*

Tan y Bwlch station is roughly halfway to Blaenau Ffestiniog and midway up the constant rising gradient; at 403 feet above Harbour station, it has long been a popular and important 'staging post' for travellers and visitors. Though this scene is from the preserved era, it has a very vintage feel. In July 1965, looking south, a selection of vintage four-wheel carriages (and one modern example at this end of the train) comprise the 'Flying flea' relief train, awaiting their return journey to Porthmadog. *Prince* has already run round and coupled to the front. Note the goods shed still in virtually original condition.

Somewhat incredibly, this is the same view, but shows just how much change has been made over the ensuing four decades. On a dull 11 June 2012 the present-day *Earl of Merioneth* waits for the road with the 1510 Blaenau Ffestiniog-Porthmadog service as *Lyd* enters with an up PTG Tours special. Tracks in the station complex are now reduced to two; there is fencing to protect the public; a footbridge now spans the tracks; and the goods shed has now been converted into a very welcome and welcoming café. *Norman Pearce, Howard Wilson collection/MJS*

The layout, appearance and function of the converted goods shed has changed considerably over the past 60 years, with ideas of what to present to the public evolving together with demands and trends. By August 1972 it is well patronised, with warm sunshine bringing out shorts and casual clothing as the visitors wait for the next train. The café door is wide open but it is purely an eatery and does not contain a booking office, hence the sign outside informing travellers to obtain 'tickets from Guard'.

Forty years later there has been yet more development. The outside tables are now more substantial, there is a covered annexe to the café, the entrance has been widened, and an extension has been built to the rear. At lunchtime on 12 June 2012, between trains, the atmosphere is relaxed as the visitors enjoy their surroundings. *Norman Pearce, Howard Wilson collection/MJS*

As well as the café, the lineside and track have also seen variations in thought. In August 1972 a smart blue VW 'Beetle' stands on the ground between building and track, while *Moelwyn* engages in a spell of shunting, controlled from the ground frame on the right. A photographer has his camera at the ready inside the white fencing.

Again, 40 years on more modern changes are considerable, with a children's playground now occupying the old siding space, the covered eating area and the rear extension plain to see, and the trackwork rationalised and simplified. On 13 June 2012 *Merddin Emrys* arrives with the 1015 service from Porthmadog, bound for Blaenau Ffestiniog, with all today's signalling and pointwork electrically controlled. *Norman Pearce, Howard Wilson collection/MJS*

The layout and provision of the station itself has also undergone continuing reappraisal. On the day of the railway's AGM in 1966, the layout was largely as inherited, with the exception of the clearance of grass around the tracks and, even more positively, refreshments being served from the 'bunny hutch'. Three lucky individuals are enjoying a ride in *Prince*'s tender as the loco runs round its train. Again the weather is shirt-sleeve order.

Three years later, in March 1969, the right-hand running line has been slewed to come closer to the 1873 booking office, which now houses a ladies' toilet. Rudimentary fencing separates the car park from the station, which now has the basics laid for a proper island platform. All attention seems to be across the valley – even the dog looks that way – and perhaps the anticipation is the imminent arrival of a train. Note the siding that snakes between the trees from a trailing point at the north end of the station.

Now into the 21st century, more developments are obvious. The platform is well-established, with seating and flower tubs; an old-style signal post has been erected, as has a signal box (upper left); the 1873 building has been given a smart lick of paint; and on the left the stone support for a new footbridge has been erected, ready to accept the bridge (seen in the background) just eight days later. *Vale of Ffestiniog* drifts into the station with the 1020 Blaenau Ffestiniog-Porthmadog service on 6 May 2012. *Peter Arnold/Norman Pearce, Howard Wilson collection/MJS*

Before... A view from the 1971-vintage, John Player Tobacco-sponsored footbridge shows the station in fuller glory, with signage, seating, flower tubs and long trains. On 2 May 1997, during yet another Bank Holiday weekend celebration, *Earl of Merioneth*, with its angular tanks, pauses with a Blaenau Ffestiniog-Porthmadog train and waits for the token to proceed. Note the proliferation of foliage on the left.

...and after! Superficially the view is the same, but we now see that the undergrowth to the left has been pruned during recent work and we have a new footbridge over the platform. Intended to recreate an earlier facility, it was as yet not open to the public when seen on Wednesday 13 June 2012. On the left, *Merddin Emrys* waits to restart the 1150 Blaenau Ffestiniog-Porthmadog roster, while an up service, hauled by *Earl of Merioneth*, begins its northward climb. *Both MJS*

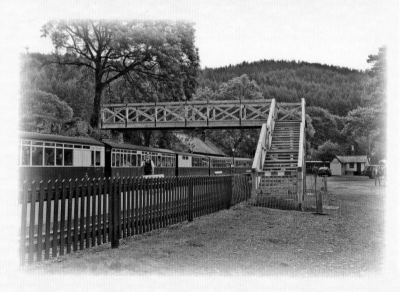

More comparative views on the ground. The original layout at Tan y Bwlch inherited by the FR in 1954 is still in situ, complete with grass, in this view from 1962. The old siding is chocked, to prevent unplanned access; *Merddin Emrys* is in its short-term, pre-1963 mode; the crew chat to enthusiastic visitors; and the crowd seems to be experiencing typical British summer weather!

By December 1969 the station platform, created the previous year, is in place, with simple fencing and a 'clock face' train announcement system. A trench is in the process of being excavated to accommodate cables for the colour light signalling scheme.

Yet more change: the date is 11 June 2012 and the new steel-boned but wooden-faced footbridge is in place, though not yet in use. The 1510 Blaenau Ffestiniog-Porthmadog service stands in the platform behind *Earl of Merioneth* (out of sight to the left). The outline of the distant hillside is constant throughout, but it is now liberally coated with trees, losing its somewhat bare appearance of yesteryear. *John Gilks/ Norman Pearce, Howard Wilson collection/MJS*

One of the delights of Tan y Bwlch in the early years of the FR was the presence of Bessie Jones, the station mistress. Appearing in traditional Welsh costume, she provided an 'extra' for the visitor to the site and had countless photographs taken over the years. Here she poses for another 'one for the album' on 30 July 1961, standing alongside the recently renamed *Earl of Merioneth*. Notice the open nature of the station so beloved of visitors at the time and much yearned for since, as well as the very neat parking. *Mike Smith*

Sadly, the photographer left no record of this shot, so although the location is obvious the working and the date are very much open to speculation, although it is some time between 1958 and 1961. Double-Fairlie *Taliesin* draws its train up alongside the 1873 building before coming forward to refresh the water tanks.

By the time of the 13 June 2012 view, there have been several versions of water tower (on the extreme left); a garden has been created between the current tank and the old building; there is now a platform, properly paved; and the 40-year-old but unused signal box dominates the right-hand side. *Merddin Emrys* similarly pauses, with the 1335 departure from Porthmadog, before having a drink. *John Wilkins, Bryan Boskett collection/MJS*

On display is a wooden replica of a short length of original 1836 track. *MJS*

On 30 July 1961 Tan y Bwlch station still retains its rural and pastoral feel, with the relaxing atmosphere at the terminus, as it then was, welcome to all. The original *Earl of Merioneth* stands by the water tower for its tanks to be replenished, watched by families and enthusiasts.

In April 1965 the tower and tank above are still in use and here provide sustenance to *Merddin Emrys*, the procedure watched by a visitor as he chats to the driver.

Ringing the changes, we now have *Linda* with a thirst and being refreshed from a later incarnation of water tower on 29 May 1970. To provide greater capacity to meet increasing demands, the old road tanker was brought in and lowered onto a pile of old sleepers on 12 May 1969. This was eventually replaced with a return to the look of the 1965 structure, seen above. *Mike Smith/Roy Wakeford/Ray Ruffell, Silver Link archive*

The climb from Tan y Bwlch to Garnedd shows just how far the railway is above the valley floor and gives some idea of the extent of the climb from Porthmadog. Also clear is the very narrow shelf on which the train is running, and the incredible achievement of the builders of the original line. On 1 September 1968 *Blanche* works hard as she approaches the Garnedd Tunnel mouth on her way to the new terminus at Dduallt, opened on 6 April that year.

Just under a year later *Mountaineer*, the motive power charged with a similar journey, has passed through the 60-yard tunnel and attacks the 1 in 85 gradient on 9 August 1969. Again the steep sides of the valley and the limited space for the railway are clear. When originally constructed in 1836 the line actually veered around the outcrop – following the line of the telegraph poles – the tunnel only being provided later in the 1850s! *Both Peter Arnold*

The incline of the hillside and the railway's audacity in carving its way onto this narrow shelf in 1836 are again evident in this view. An S&T special consisting of *Moelwyn* and wagon No 63, built for the First World War and still in service nearly 100 years later, is temporarily parked on the line on a bright day in 1962 as Norman Gurley undertakes some work with a few of his young volunteers. It would appear that a new telegraph pole is being 'planted'.

The same location ten years later, in April 1972, is graced with a much more professional assemblage, although the motive power – *Alastair* – does not look to be much of a progression! Again young volunteers are making the most of accessing such a remote location. *Both Norman Pearce, Howard Wilson collection*

A further half-mile climb from Garnedd takes the railway around a sweeping left-hand curve to Coed y Bleddiau, where the line swings hard right and strikes east. A short embankment precedes arrival at an isolated house, rumoured to have been occupied at some time before the Second World War by the pro-Nazi William Joyce, aka 'Lord Haw-Haw'. The house can just be glimpsed among the trees beyond the last coach on 9 August 1969, as *Mountaineer* enjoys the downward gradient on its way back to Porthmadog from Dduallt.

Taking time out during a lunch break on 23 April 2000, a member of the drain gang working on the brief straight length of track near Coed y Bleddiau captured this stunning panorama, beautifully portraying some of the majesty and splendour that appeals to and impresses so many travellers on the railway – a palette to delight any artist with its delightful array of hues and tints.

Peter Arnold/Tammy Stretton

Another half-mile brings the railway to Tank Curve, so named after the water tank that stands alongside the track by the curve. Situated just south of Campbell's Platform, this was the scene on 30 July 1961, with pride of place taken by the permanent way bothy. This later deteriorated and was restored by the Upper Thames Group in the late 1980s. Though the hinterland here is more undulating, the small stone embankment shows that the railway builders still did not have it easy as they crafted their way south at the constant down gradient.

Seen from the carriage window of a train bound for Blaenau Ffestiniog, the water tank stands to the left of the middle green and cream coach as *Merddin Emrys* rounds the curve and approaches Campbell's Platform on 18 May 1993.

With Campbell's Platform behind the photographer and looking back towards Garnedd, the eponymous tank can be seen by the curve in October 1964. The rusty rails, some rotting wooden sleepers and grass nearly to rail level highlight that passenger trains have not yet reached this point, with any rail traffic being merely works trains. *Mike Smith/MJS/John Wilkins, Bryan Boskett collection*

It was to be ten years between the reopening to Tan y Bwlch and the return of service trains to Dduallt, a mere 2½ miles further on! Due to a number of factors, it was neverthele frustrating for all concerned, not lea the visitors and volunteers who wish to experience 'the next stage'. Finall reopening on 6 April 1968, it was effectively a single-line branch from Tan y Bwlch for the first six weeks, v a siding in place at the station to ho a loco that would return the train to Tan y Bwlch. An operational loop wa finally completed and commissioned Approaching the station and running on what was virtually the last stretc the old line before the later reopeni beyond Tanygrisiau, *Mountaineer* is overstretched with its load of seven coaches on 31 May 1986.

Seven years later, on 2 May 1993, *Merddin Emrys* goes one better as it climbs the 1 in 85 gradient with eigh coaches on the final yards up to the station forming the 1245 Porthmado Blaenau Ffestiniog service, running 4 minutes late. *John Morgan, MJS collection/M*

Dduallt station has had various modes of announcing itself since the railway inherited the site; even before restoration here was achieved, there were the remains of the old company's sign. With the rails seemingly running through parkland, with trees flourishing in their undisturbed location, the signboard would not have been of much help to unknowledgeable visitors when photographed in October 1964!

Although the station can only be reached by train or by foot, with no road access anywhere near, its appearance to visitors has not been overlooked by the railway. As seen on 13 June 2012, with rain threatening, all is now neat and tidy with a sturdy slate shelter for the waiting traveller or passing hiker, another product of the Upper Thames Group. The start of the sharp curve at the far left is the final point of the old alignment, with the passage onto the 'deviation' tracking to the right. *John Wilkins, Bryan Boskett collection/MJS*

The modern station sign painted by volunteers. *MJS*

With the tunnel on the old route flooded by a reservoir, the railway was faced with a dilemma, which was solved by creating a spiral at Dduallt to take the line to a higher elevation for the onward run towards Tanygrisiau. Arriving on 29 July 1991 with a train from Blaenau Ffestiniog bound for Porthmadog, *Mountaineer* glides off the so-called 'deviation' back onto the original trackbed. The higher alignment can just be seen through the trees above the second coach.

A not so common sight is a train in the loop at Dduallt. On 18 June 2007 members of a party from Imperial College Railway Society are enjoying their privileged visit moments before returning south behind *Criccieth Castle*. The small headboard celebrates the passing of 175 years since the formation of the original Festiniog Railway Company by Act of Parliament on 23 May 1832. *Both MJS*

Two years after rejoining the operating railway, Dduallt station has settled into a routine, which was, at this point, for trains to terminate and allow time for passengers to wander around the decidedly peaceful site. On 29 May 1970, viewed from the hill alongside the station, *Linda* waits patiently for her travellers to regain their seats to return south. Construction of the 'deviation' is ongoing, as can be seen by the yet-be-completed bridge over the running line that will eventually take the line further on.

The passage of four decades has seen little disturbance to the station and its surroundings, other than the hillside in the foreground becoming more overgrown and a hazard to the unwary out for a stroll, with tussocks of coarse grass and very uneven ground. At 1115 on 13 June 2012 the morning's rain is passing and the sun is trying to break through the clouds, enhancing the inherent attraction of the locale. *Ray Ruffell, Silver Link archive/MJS*

Ever a delightful sight, even for those who have witnessed it before, is the spectacle of the train that you have just alighted from running over the line on which you have just arrived! Demonstrating the appeal – and far-sightedness of the 'deviationists' – on 13 June 2012 *Merddin Emrys* gathers speed as it climbs away from the station with the 1015 Porthmadog-Blaenau Ffestiniog service. *MJS*

Construction of the spiral began in 1965, three years before services would again reach this point. An imaginative scheme, it is doubly impressive in that it was created by the railway's volunteers, many of whom had no prior association with the railway but relished the challenge of this civil engineering project in a beautiful location, and gave up many long hours during the construction period to fashion this 'wonder'. The plaque says it all: 'F.R. LLYN YSTRADAU DEVIATION. CONSTRUCTION BEGAN NEAR THIS POINT ON JAN 2 1965. G. D. FOX Engineer.' *MJS*

These two views show the spiral in the making. The bridge needed to take the railway onto its higher elevation by a ruling gradient without sharp changes is here under construction. The footbridge that had formerly crossed the old line close by was demolished and replaced by a flat crossing some yards closer to Blaenau, near the house 'Rhoslyn'.

On 25 May 1969 normal services, only restored the previous year, are suspended temporarily to allow the heightening work. The receiving embankment is taking shape beyond, overlooked by the long-standing farmer's barn, and a cutting has been carved into the hillside.

Seen on the same day just beyond Barn Cutting are the preparations for the embankment needed to take the railway onwards. *Both Peter Arnold*

Without an enormous amount of help and encouragement by Colonel Campbell of Dduallt Manor – and his gunpowder licence! – the creation of the 'deviation' would have been so much harder. This plaque at Dduallt recognises his contribution. *MJS*

IN MEMORY OF
COL. ANDREW CAMPBELL
OF DDUALLT MANOR
FRIEND OF THE
FFESTINIOG RAILWAY
CYFAILL I
RHEILFFORDD FFESTINIOG
21.6.1911 - 24.2.1982

This most unusual shot of Dduallt was captured from the new higher alignment at a time when trees had not grown to shield the view. To see two locomotives at Dduallt is uncommon, but three is extremely rare. On 26 March 1983 we are treated to views of *Linda* on a train that can now travel all the way to Blaenau Ffestiniog, while *Prince* and *Moelwyn* engage in their different duties. The wooden building in the foreground was a 13-lever signal box that controlled movements for some years after 1977, until taken out of service on 15 July 1988. *John Morgan, MJS collection*

We have seen the sharp curve to the spiral from the station, but now have the view from the north end, looking back towards Tan y Bwlch on 13 June 2012. The footpath marks the route of the original line, which was abandoned after the decision to go higher to avoid the reservoir. The track was not actually lifted, however, until the 1980s. *MJS*

The course of the old line can still be followed, right up to the mouth of the old Moelwyn Tunnel, although most of the stretch is now under the control of a local farmer. On 13 June 2012 remains of the old wooden sleepers are still in situ! *MJS*

Evidence that trains once ran this way and that the rails had not been lifted so far back in history is given by yet more sleepers on the walk towards the tunnel mouth. Members of a course run by Eileen Clayton and Michael Seymour at Plas Tan y Bwlch pause to let others catch up on the old trackbed between Dduallt and the south end of the tunnel on 29 July 1991. Sebastian, the dog, a long-time favourite amongst the railway staff and volunteers, patiently succumbs to yet more attention.

The original FR footbridge over the railway – the last one still in situ when seen in the earlier picture – has been dismantled by the farmer who owns the ground, a victim of its decrepitude and modern safety concerns. This is the comparative view on 13 June 2012. The past 21 years have not been kind to the railway's memory here! *Both MJS*

This flank of the Moelwyns is syenite – a particularly hard rock – and the tunnel bored through it for the railway was thus restricted in height and width, providing little space around loco and carriages. Conditions in the tunnel were often very wet and smoky and not at all pleasant for crew, workers or passengers. In October 1964 the railway no longer runs through the tunnel, the line on the far side now being under water, but the rails still cling to their home.

The comparative scene on 13 June 2012 is obviously the same place, with Moel-yr-hydd looming in the background, but the trackbed and retaining walls have not fared well. Note that the telegraph pole still stands sentinel, but without wires! *John Wilkins, Bryan Boskett collection/MJS*

Here is another view at Tunnel South on 13 June 2012, the wider vista including, on the left, the current footpath that was once part of the original trackbed, providing a double incline to skirt the mountain flank in the days before the tunnel was built by 1844. *MJS*

Moving to the top of the incline seen in the previous picture, this is the view in the opposite direction in October 1964, with track still in place on the railway embankment in the middle of the vale. *John Wilkins, Bryan Boskett collection*

Despite climbing from the original elevation, the railway was once again forced to drill through apparently solid rock on the upper flank of the Moelwyns during the late 1970s. A sizeable camp was established to blast and drill, and transfer the rock spoil to create the necessary passage for the railway. While the stratum was almost as tough as that faced by their ancestors,

the 'deviationists' enjoyed modern machinery and managed to create an envelope that was considerably greater than the old tunnel. With the old incline just visible to the right on 14 November 1976, on the left is a spoil train. The Buchan skips on the central line proved to be unstable, being top-heavy and tipping their loads onto the poor track!

Another angle on the construction site on the same day features *Diana* at the head of a train of graded microsyenite. The tunnel mouth can just be seen in the right distance. Mist looks as though it is about to descend from the mountain tops. *Both Howard Wilson*

We are through, and trains can negotiate the tunnel. In 1978 *Blanche* emerges from the southern portal on a return run from the new terminus at Tanygrisiau. Note the concrete lining to the tunnel – shotcreted over the previous winter – and the larger envelope allowing for the bigger locomotives and carriages than used by the original railway, and a requirement under modern conditions. *Norman Pearce, Howard Wilson collection*

What a sight! *Merddin Emrys* bursts forth into Tunnel North Cutting, between Dduallt and Tanygrisiau, on 25 June 1977, the first train to break through this barrier, proudly boasting 'Blaenau Ffestiniog here we come!'. Despite all the doom-mongers and naysayers in former years, when the plans were laid to return to Blaenau Festiniog, the railway had proved it possible and this day was one of many to celebrate on this last push to the ultimate goal. *FR Co, Norman Gurley, MJS collection*

A quick look ahead sees *Prince* and *Conway Castle* double-heading the 1300 Blaenau Ffestiniog-Porthmadog service, some 40 minutes late as it passes Llyn Ystradau on 2 May 1993. In the foreground the 1836 incline plane on the north side of the Moelwyns is clear to see, as is, on the right, the 1844 trackbed to the old tunnel, both visible due to the very low level of the reservoir. *MJS*

Photographs of the railway in situ on the old tunnel's northern approach are not so common, especially one showing the turnout for the branch to Brooke's Quarry. Thus this view from Easter 1952 is very welcome, showing that the retaining walls are in good state despite the railway having been closed for six years, and the track looks as though it only needs a weedkilling train to pass! *David Morgan*

In another view of the Eileen Clayton/Michael Seymour course on 29 July 1991, the participants are invited to savour the water being so low in the reservoir and enjoy the view across to the tunnel mouth in the fold of the hillside at the end of the raised trackbed. Some, however, are seemingly more interested in what is happening on the main running line above! *MJS*

Again looking at the railway as it passes the Llyn Ystradau reservoir – the reason why the railway was built to the higher level – *Earl of Merioneth* heads for home with the 1155 departure from Blaenau Ffestiniog on 5 March 2000. The old trackbeds are once more in view to the trained eye, though partly hidden by the water. *Tammy Stretton*

We have now crossed and climbed above the railway, and 1979-vintage *Earl of Merioneth* is seen heading downhill past the reservoir, with the site of the temporary Llyn Ystradau platform just behind the final carriage. The date is 3 May 2004 and the pumped-storage lake is full. The footpath to the right of the train is once more the 1836 alignment of the original railway. *MJS*

For a little under
a year, as the
work continued to
prepare Tanygrisiau
to become the next
northern terminus,
there was a
temporary terminal
arrangement
alongside Llyn
Ystradau. In this
undated view, *Linda*
is about to pass
the site of that
short-term facility,
heading instead for
Tanygrisiau.

Swinging round
to follow the
passage of the
train, we see the
power station,
sitting squarely
across the old
trackbed. *Both John
Gilks*

Running on the old trackbed at Llyn Ystradau, Double-Fairlie *Merddin Emrys* leaves Tanygrisiau on 29 May 1936 and negotiates the narrow rock shelf. To the right is the alignment of the original 1836 formation. The loco is on what is now the road to the power station, while the present-day track goes behind the rock outcrop on the left and passes between the two houses in the background, closer to the waterfall.

Although the image is not dated, the headboard – 'The First New Fairlie Built Since 1911' – gives a clue, *Earl of Merioneth* having been new from Boston Lodge in 1979. In what is presumably one of its earliest runs, it passes behind the power station, on the new higher trackbed, on its way to the then terminus at Tanygrisiau. *R. Piercy, MJS collection/ Norman Gurley, FR Archives, MJS collection*

When considering the position regarding returning trains to Tanygrisiau, the railway was faced with a major problem. With the approach now being substantially higher than the original trackbed and the onward journey from there to Blaenau Ffestiniog being on the original route, the discrepancy between the two levels needed creative solutions. The answer was in crossing the Stwlan Dam access road on the level, then raising the shelf of the actual station by around 3 feet, to allow for a gentle and smooth descent. On 14 August 1992 *Mountaineer* coasts down this gradient and crosses the road with what was by then a regular service travelling the full length of the route.

Three years later, on 20 August 1995, *David Lloyd George* is in charge of the reverse working, the fireman taking a brief rest as the loco crosses the road watched by another enthusiast. Note the warning lights for both road and rail. *Both John Morgan*

The changed levels meant blasting rock from the Tanygrisiau station site, and the result can be seen on 9 July 1978, when the station was a temporary terminus. Note also the installation of a new bridge across the waterfall outflow in the foreground, as *Linda* runs round her train. Note how the railway curves around the rocky outcrop, another result of the new approach compared to the original, which had a much straighter trajectory on the right of this view. *R. Fisher, MJS collection*

Now down on the ground, the substantial extent of the work to carve out a way through the rocks and between the houses becomes clear. In this undated view from 1976, a variety of machines are on site, as a small knot of individuals consider the size of the task ahead. Passengers were able to travel into Tanygrisiau again within two years.

Using a slightly wider-angle lens shows the results of the railway's handiwork over the ensuing 26 years. On 11 June 2012 a couple wait patiently at the shelter for the next down train, while enjoying the peaceful and quiet surroundings. Note the extension to the white cottage on the right, and the way that nature has healed the scars of the railway's work by the growth of trees. *Howard Wilson/MJS*

As can be seen in the lower picture, Tanygrisiau station is of an island design, with lines on either side of the central platform. This has not always been the case, however, although originally constructed in this fashion for the 1978 opening. Once the line was finally extended to its goal at Blaenau Ffestiniog, the run-round loop at Tanygrisiau was no longer required and was removed. This is the state on 29 July 1991 as *Merddin Emrys* reaches the station with the morning departure from Porthmadog. Note how both the railway and the white cottage are dwarfed by the mountainous backdrop – and the lamp standard with no lamp! *MJS*

Turning round and looking towards Blaenau, this was the scene on 12 July 1980 when the station was still a terminus. *Blanche* receives some attention as she stands waiting to begin the return journey to Porthmadog after running round the train. The results of blasting still look fresh on the rocks above the second coach, and the lamps have light fittings. *MJS*

As well as popular May Day Bank Holiday weekend Galas, the railway also excels at Vintage Weekends, when past operations are (often incredibly authentically) recreated. However, not every train falls into this category, and on 26 October 1996 it is stretching the term 'vintage' a little as we see *Blanche* and *Mountaineer* (here posing as WD No 1265 in mock wartime livery) about to restart the 1350 Porthmadog-Blaenau Ffestiniog working. The tight curvature of the current platform is here well highlighted, with most of the train lost around the corner. The rails in the foreground are for reinstating the loop.

As the railway now follows right-hand running, a strict comparative view is not available under normal circumstances and trains do not always stop here. After a request stop, the fireman of *Merddin Emrys* studies some part of his charge as the 1015 Porthmadog-Blaenau Ffestiniog train restarts the climb away from Tanygrisiau on Tuesday 12 June 2012. The sole remaining building from the old station, the goods shed, stands to the left but is now some 3 feet lower in relation to the platform than of yore. *Both MJS*

The date is August 1966, the railway here has been abandoned for 20 years, and it is far from certain that trains will run this far again. The old rails are still in situ as the dog turns from its climb up the steps between the two stone walls; access for road vehicles was from the other end of the site. The old goods sheds stand alongside the left-hand car, and the pump-storage reservoir is in full operation and fully supplied on this day. The derelict ground floor of the formerly two-storey station building is beyond the goods shed.

Though self-evidently the same location, the transformation by 12 June 2012 is remarkable. Not only have the trackwork and the station site been improved, with the goods shed now lower than the platform area, but the houses on both sides of the railway have also all seen improvements, with new slates, fences, gates and even spruced-up front gardens. The view of the reservoir is now hidden by the row of conifers. *Howard Wilson/MJS*

Immediately north of Tanygrisiau station the railway crossed Dolrhedyn bridge, taking it over a very steep local road. On the assumption that the railway would not be back this way following the drowning of the original route by the reservoir, the local authority removed the bridge, leaving the chasm between tracks seen here in March 1972. The assumption that there would be no need for it to be subsequently replaced proved unfounded! With smoke from many house fires behind him, a well-stocked onion-seller is obviously hopeful of sales as he trudges up the slope!

In the winter of 1979 local authority employees were back to reinstate the bridge! Two survey the scene and discuss the next steps, only yards from Penlan, where major civil engineering was necessary before tracklaying could commence. Blaenau stands in the distance ... so close and yet so far!

With new concrete cradles and bridge base, *Earl of Merioneth* is safe to steam northwards over the new structure in August 1987. Note the arrival of new industrial units in the valley and the complete lack of chimney smoke compared to the 1972 view. *Norman Pearce, Howard Wilson collection/Tony Baker/John Gilks*

Moving back towards the station, visible in the left background, we finish our visit to Tanygrisiau with a view of 1979-vintage *Earl of Merioneth* heading north on the final short run to Blaenau Ffestiniog in August 1987, proudly displaying a 'Mountain Prince' headboard. The mountainous terrain of the area is clear from this angle, with habitation clinging to the hillside cheek-by-jowl with the railway. One hopes the spectacular view is some compensation for local residents. *MJS*

On the final approach to the terminus in Blaenau Ffestiniog the railway passes through the small village suburb of Glan y Pwll, and in this view from April 1972, during the inter-regnum years, the previous regime's tracks are just visible in the green sward as they approach Glan y Pwll house and the road crossing adjacent to it. The gates to the latter have not been disturbed for years, and neither has the rear of the property by the look of it. On the left are the skeletal remains of the railway's former engine shed; note also the massive slate waste tips that have dominated the Blaenau skyline for more than a century.

After being reclaimed by the railway, the house was converted into 'top end' headquarters for the PW/CE Department and was also used as a hostel for a time. In this view from the early 1980s, on the opposite side of the hostel from the railway and looking away from Blaenau, members of the Midland Group are supplemented by some volunteers from GPT Works in Coventry and are in the process of digging in search of the manhole for the main sewer that ran under the access here. *Norman Pearce, Howard Wilson collection/Tony Baker*

By reopening day, 25 May 1982, fencing has been renewed and the crossing at Glan y Pwll is properly controlled. Returning with the second train on the first day, the weather looks to be turning inclement as *Linda* sweeps over the road, about to pass the hostel. With no back cab, those on the footplate are likely to have a damp trip back to Porthmadog.

Moving forward 13 years to 2 July 1995, *Merddin Emrys*, with a full complement, is captured from the footbridge seen in the background in the earlier view. Note how the house and its surroundings have been tidied and improved, not least with a new boundary wall and fencing at the far end. The road is controlled by flashing lights, and the second track was laid for future plans, which have not yet come to fruition. *Peter Treloar, MJS collection/John Morgan, MJS collection*

In the inter-regnum years, access to the housing on the left from the vantage point of the photographer had been by foot crossing, but this could not be allowed after the railway returned. Thus the aforementioned new footbridge was installed, and this view is from June 1981, less than a year before rails and trains would again take this route. The railway navvies will have to work fast!

Sadly the footbridge was not to survive the passage of time and is no more. In this view from 6 May 2012 the boundary wall to the right has been lowered, allowing a better view of the housing adjacent to the PW building and the more modern development by the railway beyond. The height of the rocky backdrop is also intensified in this angle compared to the earlier picture. *Norman Pearce, Howard Wilson collection/MJS*

Once again we see a situation where the previous straight alignment of the old railway has been blocked by a stone wall following developments, in this case by road realignments. In October 1963 the break in the slate wall to the left of the extant rails marks the site of what was the old FR station, Stesion Fain, which boasted a lengthy but narrow canopy to protect waiting passengers from the bouts of wet weather at this height. The old station water tower still stands, across from the ex-LMS standard-gauge station, complete with its yellow brick adornments. The wooden LNWR/LMS building had burned down in 1951 and was replaced by the one seen here in 1956. This finally closed in 1982, when the new arrangements in the centre of Blaenau came into force with the opening of the present BR facility, adjacent to the new FR station.

The fortunes of the ex-LMS station have not been good since 1982. Its goods yards have been lost to rail traffic and the building, suffering from neglect, was taken down during 2012. Many of the yellow bricks have also gone. On the FR, a new entrance to Blaenau has been forged, with a bridge under the roadway built to accommodate double track. In this view from 6 May 2012 all traces of Stesion Fain have now been lost, with the tracks lifted in 1973 and moved to Glan y Pwll, ready for the coming of the new railway. *Norman Pearce, Howard Wilson collection/MJS*

Between the standard-gauge station on North Western Road and the centre of Blaenau Ffestiniog, the fortunes of the two railways – BR and FR – have changed more than once. In earlier times, the FR tracks ran to the left here, going into the goods yard by the LMS station. There was no connection between the LNWR/LMS and the GWR, which had arrived in the town from the opposite direction. Subsequent to closure of the ex-GWR line on 30 January 1961, a connection was made to allow nuclear flask trains to access Trawsfynydd Power Station. This connection opened in April 1964 and is seen here on the right in July of that year, with the track obviously being new. In contrast, the FR rails to the left, now out of use since 1963, look very much the worse for wear.

By June 1981 even the standard-gauge track is looking careworn, but, still in use for nuclear traffic, it will have to survive until the new tracks to what would become Blaenau Central station, out of sight to the left under the bridge, are completed. Track panels for this new arrangement can be seen under the bridge. *John Wilkins, Bryan Boskett collection/ Norman Pearce, Howard Wilson collection*

Moving closer to the heart of Blaenau and looking back on the same day in June 1981, the double concrete box that will see FR trains in less than 12 months is clearly seen, its relatively recent installation being marked by the complete lack of any reclamation by nature and the equal lack of fencing to safeguard the railway either atop or to the left on the ground. The BR track snakes to the right to go through the ex-LMS station.

By 12 June 2012 the aesthetics of the view are greatly enhanced by the smoothing of the harsh landscape by greenery. With the reopening of the FR to Blaenau in 1982, the positioning of the tracks relative to those of BR was swapped, the latter now to the right, accessing the new station (behind the photographer) but no longer carrying traffic onward to Trawsfynydd, whereas the FR rails see regular use to and from Porthmadog. One wonders whether the right-hand box for the FR's route will ever be needed! *Norman Pearce, Howard Wilson collection/MJS*

Ambitions are fulfilled and history is made. *Earl of Merioneth*, just three years old, climbs the last few yards into Blaenau Ffestiniog station on 25 May 1982, the very first FR passenger train to return to the northern terminus under the new regime, watched by enthusiastic crowds on both the FR and BR station platforms. Note the run-round loop in the BR station.

Reproducing that classic view, the very same *Earl of Merioneth* enters the station with the first train of the day on Saturday 5 May 2012, during the FR 'Blaenau 30' Gala, with the 1015 service from Porthmadog. Graced with the original celebratory headboard, it runs alongside Class 150 DMU No 150279 forming the 1022 service from Llandudno, which Arriva Trains Wales had timed to arrive simultaneously, combining diesel horn with steam whistle to add to the sense of occasion! A short cavalcade of other locos and stock is temporarily ignored as the trains arrive. Alongside, the Network Rail tracks have a rusty hue, the loop being rarely used.
Peter Treloar, MJS collection/MJS

Moments later *Earl of Merioneth* climbs the last few yards into the new Blaenau Ffestiniog FR station on 25 May 1982, with yet more excited crowds to welcome it. Note the panels on the ground waiting to be installed to extend the more permanent fencing; the ambulance in the school grounds, on hand in case of need; and the relatively few people with cameras!

The present-day comparative view was taken slightly earlier than the 1982 picture due to the subsequent construction of the waiting shelters on the FR platform otherwise obscuring the view of the steam loco. Arriva Trains Wales's Class 150 No 150279 is now closer to its destination. The train was 'solid' with passengers travelling to the occasion at Blaenau, and no doubt ATW would be happy for this situation to pertain every day! Note that by the 21st century the FR station also has a second platform. *Peter Treloar, MJS collection/MJS*

Another view from the visit of June 1981 shows the twin tracks in place in the new BR station, though not ballasted, and the platform not yet constructed. The left-hand track under the curved footbridge is that seen on page 97 but is not yet a loop, as the trains for Trawsfynydd will need it. The foreground land, where narrow-gauge and standard-gauge tracks once intermingled for transfer of traffic, is being prepared to receive the FR the following year.

Standing under the smartly painted awning on the FR station on 12 June 2012, it hardly seems possible that this is the same vantage point and angle, but such is the transformation at Blaenau over the years. All three loops are now in place and the standard-gauge platform stretches out towards the footbridge. Capable of handling a train of many carriages, the normal provision is just a two-car unit. *Norman Pearce, Howard Wilson collection/MJS*

In a depressing view from January 1967, this desolation is the result of abandonment of the area following the closure of the ex-GWR station and the ripping up of both standard-gauge and narrow-gauge tracks that once shared the open ground to the left. The station platform is on the right, and an ugly rump of a building is all that is left of its former presence. The single track still in place is that tenuous access to the nuclear power station at Trawsfynydd.

The 'past' view looks to have been taken from the old signal box, judging by its height, and this has long gone. Similarly, there has been much development over recent years, as well as tree growth, and this is as close as could be obtained for a comparative view. On 11 June 2012 the former Trawsfynydd line is in the foreground, now truncated, with the platform of the current Network Rail station visible upper centre. The alignment of the old FR track that ran behind the old GWR station is roughly echoed by that of the far side of the car park, to the right of the station. *Norman Pearce, Howard Wilson collection/MJS*

Another view from January 1967, but this time we are on the platform of the ex-GWR station, looking away from the route of our journey thus far. Through the bridge, left of centre, running under the town's main road, the old FR's final terminus at Duffws can just be spied. The route of the FR's track ran alongside the small wall on the left and through the bridge, and it hardly seems feasible that there should ever have been a railway running there! Abandoned bricks and other detritus serve to depress the view, and not even the sight of the Queen's Hotel on the right lifts the spirits.

An exact comparison is impossible due to the massive reorganisation and redevelopment over the years, but the house on the left and the Queen's Hotel are markers for orientation. The former railway bridge no longer stands and the alignment of the standard-gauge tracks does not match the earlier one. However, one has to admit that the view of 5 May 2012, showing the two present termini, is a vast improvement and far more pleasing to the eye! *Norman Pearce, Howard Wilson collection/MJS*

We are now standing underneath that main road in this view from March 1972, ten years after the cessation of slate quarry trains on the FR here, looking at the scene at Duffws that would have met the driver and fireman in the days of the railway. Passenger services to Duffws ceased in 1939, the tracks have gone and the area has been converted into a car park, but the terminus building still stands, though rather ignominiously it is now a toilet block! Again the view does not stimulate, not helped by the massive grey hillside as a backdrop.

The earlier vantage point would now be in the middle of the main road, so wishing to avoid suicide, and with more recent developments in Blaenau partly obscuring the view, this is a comparison slightly closer to the old Duffws building. The latter still serves as a convenience to the town and has car parking around it but, as can be seen, new ideas of roadways are in hand on 12 June 2012. On a slightly brighter day, the 'slate mountain' does not look so brooding. *Norman Pearce, Howard Wilson collection/MJS*

Our final view of Blaenau's stations is of the ex-GWR facility in 1960, with an ex-GWR
0-6-0PT releasing some steam as it waits to restart its rather lonely and exposed
trip from here towards Bala. The damp weather will not add to the enjoyment of
its journey. The signal box stands on the left, controlling the freight yard that was a
mixture of narrow and standard gauge, as traffic was interchanged between the two
systems. Standard-gauge Presflo cement wagons are stabled in the yard, used to supply
Trawsfynydd Nuclear Power Station.

Again, the realignment of track with the construction of the new station disguises
the previous landscape, but this view of 'little and large' is close. Funkey diesel *Vale of
Ffestiniog* stands on display alongside 'big brother' Class 59 No 59205 *L. Keith McNair*
at Blaenau on 18 April 1998. The latter has arrived with 'The Roman Nose' rail tour
– from Euston to Trawsfynydd – and both locos are in National Power colours, that
company having sponsored the initial painting of the FR's diesel. *John Wilkins, Bryan Boskett
collection/MJS*

And so we bid farewell to sunny Blaenau...! Bearing the original 'Order! Order!' headboard from 1982, *Earl of Merioneth* gathers speed as it leaves Blaenau Ffestiniog with the ten-coach 1150 to Porthmadog in the weak sunshine of Sunday 6 May 2012, as part of the 'Blaenau Ffestiniog 30' celebrations. Note that, compared to the view on page 97, the FR is now separated from its neighbours by a purpose-built stone wall. The FR looks neat and tidy compared to the rubbish that litters the standard-gauge route, and just two enthusiasts watch from the footbridge. *MJS*

PRINCESS: From the railway opening in 1836 until 1863 the operations were handled literally by gravity, powering loaded waggons of slate down the line, while horses laboriously hauled the empty stock back up the line from Porthmadog – they did get a rest riding down by gravity in the waggons. While this was initially very profitable, the sheer weight of slate and the number of trains progressively increased to the point where more powerful motive power was required. Thus four locomotives were supplied in 1863/64 by George England & Co. *Princess* became No 1 in the company's books.

Princess was originally built as an 0-4-0 side-tank loco without a cab, and named *The Princess* being subsequently converted to a saddle tank in March 1895. In recent years, this fine old lady had been on static display in Spooner's restaurant at Porthmadog. Following removal from the restaurant to Boston Lodge works, the loco was lovingly refreshed. To honour the magnificent achievement of the railway's 150th anniversary of steam operation *Princess* was then transhipped

from Wales to reside for a while on public display at Paddington station, seen here on Platform 9 on 5 March 2013. *Norman Pearce, Howard Wilson collection/MJS*

PRINCE: Delivered several months after *Princess* and becoming No 3 on the railway, *Prince* is undoubtedly the best-known of the four with the railway's operators and visitors, not least by being the first steam locomotive to be resurrected by the new regime in 1954. It has been rebuilt at least twice and has worn two liveries since then, initially appearing in plain green. The attractive lined version, seen here at Boston Lodge in July 1963, was applied after a rebuild completed in the spring of that year. The nameplate support has also changed over time. *Merddin Emrys* is in similar garb behind.

Since 1986 the favoured colour has been this slightly gaudy but nonetheless attractive shade of red, which certainly lifts the profile of the loco. On 11 August 1993 *Prince* stands over the pit in Boston Lodge yard, with *Upnor Castle* in the background at the yard mouth. Note that the nameplate is supported vertically here, as opposed to leaning towards the tank as in the earlier picture. *Norman Pearce, Howard Wilson collection/Tammy Stretton*

PALMERSTON: No 4 in the railway's books, and delivered in 1864, this loco was named after Henry John Temple, 3rd Viscount Palmerston KG GCB PC, Prime Minister (for a second stint) at the time. Out of main-line service in the 1930s, it became a stationary boiler supplying a steam hammer in the smithy at Boston Lodge and its abandoned appearance after this duty is seen on 9 July 1953, with the various pipes still attached. Without nameplate, but with a Boston Lodge rebuild plate still affixed to the cabside, it has obviously not moved for some considerable time!

Unlike *Prince*, *Palmerston* has carried a single livery of lined maroon since restoration in 1993. Proving wrong the naysayers, who doubted it would ever be returned to steam, it now gives good service on vintage trains and special occasions, and here stands at the head of a Colonel Stephens Society 'jolly' at Minffordd on 19 May 2012. *Peter Gray, MJS collection/Judi Stretton*

WELSH PONY: For a change we now travel much further back in time for the 'past' view, witnessing *Welsh Pony* speeding up Gwyndy Bank in the mid-1930s with an up train, and wearing a sun-bleached green livery, a consequence of using the wrong sort of paint!. Considering the speed of film and the less sophisticated cameras then available, the photographer has done really well to keep the loco very close to sharp focus while the embankment is blurred in the panning. The driver casually perches on the vacuum brake cylinder, just inside the back of the cab, as his charge forges onward.

New in 1867, again from George England & Co, *Welsh Pony* was another loco to survive the abandonment of 1946, albeit having been taken out of service in 1939, but this time has not seen restoration, although attention has been given to the project from time to time. It has spent various periods on display in some form or other, and is seen here on 2 July 1999 on a plinth at the entrance to the car park at Harbour station. *MJS collection/John Morgan, MJS collection*

MERDDIN EMRYS:
Although the England 0-4-0s – there had been six in service by 1867 – fulfilled their roles with credit, the continual increase in traffic and loads led to investigations for more powerful motive power, and 1869 saw the introduction of *Little Wonder*. This the first of a new design of patent double engine from Robert Fairlie, having one long boiler with two central fireboxes and driving controls, and with an 0-4-4-0T arrangement. Though scrapped in 1882, the design had been proven; *James Spooner* followed in 1872, then *Merddin Emrys* seven years later. Named after a sixth-century Welsh bard, sometimes also known as King Arthur's wizard Merlin, the loco has become one of the most successful of the railway's fleet and it is not unusual for it to cover more miles per year than its stablemates. Like any steam locomotive, it needs constant attention and regular overhauls, and it is in process of this over the ash pit in Boston Lodge yard on 13 July 1963.
   With a major rebuild in 1987/88 behind it, *Merddin* was back in steam in 2005, as an oil-burner, before being converted back to coal-firing over the winter of 2006/07. In fine form, it leaves Tan y Bwlch on 13 June 2012 after a stop with the 1150 Blaenau Ffestiniog-Porthmadog service, in the colour that has become its norm. *Mike Smith/MJS*

LIVINGSTON THOMPSON:
The identity of this
locomotive has
transmogrified on several
occasions during its
lifetime, and its precise
state at any one moment
can be confusing for the
inexpert. Built in 1886 as
Livingston Thompson, named
after the Chairman and
Managing Director of the
Festiniog Railway Company,
it has also masqueraded
as *Taliesin* and *Earl of
Merioneth*. In addition, to
add to the confusion, it
was renumbered No 3 in
1887, after being allocated
the number 11 by the
company when new! In
undercoat grey, following
restoration by the new
regime, it is watched (by
the photographer's wife?)
shunting at the mouth of
Boston Lodge yard in early
1957.

Renamed *Earl of
Merioneth* in 1961, in an
attempt to garner publicity
from the gift of that title to
the Duke of Edinburgh by
the Queen – and the railway
runs mainly through the old
county of Merionethshire
– it was painted green, as
seen here by the coaling
stage at Harbour station
on 26 March 1967.

Withdrawn from active
service in 1971, in 1988 it
was sent for preservation
and display at the
National Railway Museum,
York, reunited with its
Livingston Thompson
nameplates. With that
name it has briefly escaped
incarceration to be on
show at Harbour station
on 30 April 2005. *John Wilkins,
Bryan Boskett collection/Peter Arnold/
MJS*

EARL OF MERIONETH:
1979 was a momentous year for the FR Fairlies. It was the centenary of the entry into traffic of *Merddin Emrys*, **and in March the Board gave favourable consideration for the old loco that had been** *Earl of Merioneth* **to go to the NRM in York. Three months later Boston Lodge saw the steaming of a brand-new Double-Fairlie** *Earl of Merioneth*, **the first of its type for many years, to be formally named by General Manager Allan Garraway on 23 June.**

Though built to the classic Festiniog Fairlie design, there was some consternation and outcry that the new loco did not fit easily into the family with its angular tanks. This view at Blaenau Ffestiniog on 29 April 2005 clearly portrays this feature.

The 1979-built *Earl of Merioneth* **has been green throughout its life, though the precise hue has varied slightly and it has borne several designs of lining and panelling. Initially equipped with plain, square-profile dome covers, it now carries much rounder, polished brass examples, as seen here when it was just out of the works after overhaul on 1 January 2008; bearing the all-over black applied to all locos while running in, it stands in pouring rain with Single-Fairlie** *Taliesin* **at Blaenau.** *MJS/Tammy Stretton*

DAVID LLOYD GEORGE is named after the man regarded as perhaps having made a greater impact on British public life than any other 20th-century leader, due to his leadership during the First World War, his post-war role in reshaping Europe, and his introduction of Britain's social welfare system before the war; he is also the only British Prime Minister to have been Welsh (though born in Manchester, the family returned to Wales when he was just two months old) and to have spoken English as a second language. As he lived for many years at Llanystumdwy, Caernarfonshire, and was articled to a solicitor in Portmadoc, the decision to name the latest loco from Boston Lodge *Dafydd Lloyd George/David Lloyd George* – bilingually on both sides of the loco – was wholly appropriate. New out of the works when seen on 6 August 1992 and the most powerful locomotive on the railway, it wears the usual initial plain black livery as it is still incomplete.

Standing proud and confident on the pit in Boston Lodge Works yard on 4 June 1995, *DLG*, as it is affectionately known, seems to be aware of its status within the fleet, looking magnificent in its individual livery of yellow-and-black-lined China Red, though the Boston Lodge wags swiftly dubbed it 'tomato soup' in a typically jesting allusion to the offering in the café at the other end of the Cob! *Tammy Stretton/MJS*

TALIESIN: **The last loco from Boston Lodge built to a Victorian FR design, the brand-new *Taliesin*, again in initial plain black livery, approaches Minffordd on 1 May 1999, with bunting out and crowds waving for its first public run, as the 1130 Porthmadog-Tan y Bwlch service. Utilising the reversing lever, chimney and front lamp iron from the original 1876-vintage loco that had been scrapped in 1935, but otherwise new, it recreated the original Single-Fairlie. The name is that of another sixth-century Welsh bard.**

After the early runs in black, *Taliesin* was graced with a very attractive maroon lake livery lined with straw and grey. Standing in the yard at Boston Lodge on 29 April 2005, the bright early afternoon sunshine picks out the details and sinuous curves of the loco to perfection. *Both MJS*

LINDA: The early 1960s saw the FR struggling to juggle increases in traffic demands with a loco fleet that was too small and/or worn out. Seeking solutions, one answer came in the guise of 0-4-0ST *Linda* from Penrhyn Quarry. Initially merely on loan, this lady was not for returning and she stayed! Arriving on the FR on 15 July 1962 as an 0-4-0ST, without a tender, she had been new from the Hunslet Engine Co in Leeds in 1893 and was named after the daughter of the 3rd Baron Penrhyn. Her term in the quarry in North Wales was just short of 70 years and, although built for heavy works on the main line of the PQR, she has certainly seen her fair share of labour since joining the FR, having covered many more miles in the last 60 years than she ever did in the previous 70!

For the majority of her time on the FR, *Linda* has run with an open-backed cab, offering the crew little shelter from the elements, especially when running in reverse. However, when seen on 28 August 1999, in glorious black lined livery, she is giving her crew greater protection, although the sun is shining!

She has had a variety of coats, including blue, but is seen in the third picture in black and green, running once again without a cab cover, and unusually 'cadging a lift', working home with *Earl of Merioneth* on the 1150 Blaenau Ffestiniog-Porthmadog service on 5 May 2012. *Norman Pearce, Howard Wilson collection/Judi Stretton/MJS*

BLANCHE: Named after the Hon Blanche Georgiana Fitzroy, wife of the 3rd Baron Penrhyn and mother of Linda, the railway sister to *Linda* also served a little short of 70 years on the Penrhyn Quarry Railway and is seen here on that railway, at Port Penrhyn, outside the railway's headquarters. Again seen as originally built as an 0-4-0ST, this time with basic cab back-sheet, she too was converted, in 1972, to an 2-4-0ST after both she and *Linda* demonstrated a little instability on FR tracks without the pony truck. She is obviously well cared for by her crew here.

At Boston Lodge yard in April 1967 Blanche is in glorious green lined livery and complete with the much fuller protection for the crew, with the fully enclosed cab back. Four years after transfer from Penrhyn she is burning coal but, like *Linda*, would be converted to oil. Her wheel arrangement conversion in 1972 utilised a wheel set from *Moel Tryfan*, a loco long extinct from the old Welsh Highland Railway. As seen here she is still with slide valves.

MJS collection/Norman Pearce, Howard Wilson collection

MOUNTAINEER: An American Locomotive Co product – affectionately known on the FR as 'The ALCO' – *Mountaineer* was new in 1917, built for use by the British Army during the First World War. Having worked in France after the war, on the Tramway de Pithiviers à Toury until the early 1960s, it was eventually purchased by FR supporter John Ransom in mid-decade. In as-delivered condition, with the ancient 'Long Shed' as backdrop, the initially anonymous loco is being prepared in Boston Lodge yard in March 1969. It was to see more than one re-evaluation of final design over the years.

In one of its early incarnations, in lined green livery, at Harbour station in October 1983, *Mountaineer* has a revised cab, remodelled domes, a shortened chimney and extended smokebox, together with a front headlamp bearing the 'ALCO' legend. Steam is raised prior to making a foray up the line. *Norman Pearce, Howard Wilson collection/John Morgan, MJS collection*

The maker's plate, showing who, where and when, together with the relevant works number. *MJS collection*

LYD: The latest new-build at the time of writing, *Lyd* is unashamedly recreating the Manning Wardle locomotives built for the Lynton & Barnstaple Railway in the early years of the 20th century. The brainchild of James Evans, he almost single-handedly pushed the project forward in the early stages before it was accepted into the Boston Lodge workflow and inherited by the FR. New in 2010, again in unlined black livery, it has already proved its worth despite its small 2-6-2T appearance. On its first day in steam it comes alive on Sunday 2 May 2010 during the FR's 'Quirks & Curiosities' Gala. Standing in Boston Lodge yard, it whistles in triumph. *Lyd* carries two variants of cab design – nearest the camera a cut-down FR version and, on the far side, the L&B profile. They are interchangeable, depending on the railway on which the loco is operating!

After running for a while in unlined black, lined black, and Southern green livery, *Lyd* was allocated a number in addition to its name as one of the SR-inherited class of Manning Wardles, and was repainted in a wholly imaginary BR lined black, mixed-traffic livery. As BR No 30190 it reaches the final few yards on the approach to Tan y Bwlch station on 25 April 2011 with the 0945 Porthmadog-Tan y Bwlch vintage shuttle. Note the 'cow catcher' on the front buffer beam. *Both MJS*

LILLA: Built by the Hunslet Engine Co and supplied to Cilgwyn Quarry, near Nantlle in North Wales, in 1891 as an 0-4-0ST, it is not, historically, from the old FR. In 1928 it was sold to the Penrhyn Quarry Railway for £150 and moved to its new home via the WHR (Bryngwyn-Dinas) and LMS (on a standard-gauge wagon from Dinas to Port Penrhyn). In many ways an enlarged version of smaller locos from this builder, it seems to have been something of a one-off. Bought privately in 1963, it was eventually acquired by a consortium connected with the FR in 1997, after coming to Boston Lodge for the Hunslet Hundred Gala in 1995 and a subsequent overhaul. She is seen at Minffordd on 15 March 2009. A common name in north-east Sicily, the precise origin of *Lilla*'s name is a mystery. *Judi Stretton*

BRITOMART: Named after a nymph of Greek mythology and a character from *The Faerie Queene*, *Britomart* is yet another ex-quarry loco – from the Pen-yr-Orsedd quarry, where it spent its entire working life – that is finding a new and useful home on the FR, though privately owned. Again from Hunslet, Leeds, in 1899, it enjoys occasional excursions up the line, often to spend time entertaining the visitors at a particular location or on a special occasion, as here at Blaenau Ffestiniog during a Gala on 25 April 2011. Its unusual blue coat, based on the Caledonian Railway livery, is a welcome variation from the rest of the fleet. *MJS*

MARY ANN, the first engine to work on the revived Ffestiniog Railway in 1954, was another loco built for British Army use during the First World War, this time by Motor Rail, a Bedford-based locomotive builder formed in 1911. Bought by the old FR in 1923, she has been undertaking unsung, largely engineering duties ever since and is probably the longest-serving internal-combustion locomotive on any operational railway. Operating a shuttle between yard and station, she passes the weigh house at Minffordd on 3 May 1999, the third day of another FR Gala. *MJS*

MOELWYN is yet another survivor of the Great War – built as an 0-4-0 petrol loco by Baldwin for the French Army in 1918 – and was bought by the original FR in 1925, but this time for slightly heavier duties than those allocated to *Mary Ann*. Various refinements have been made to the loco over the past five decades, including the fitting of a pony truck, a change of wheel arrangement to 2-4-0, and the fitting of a diesel engine. It is seen here in its more recent incarnation in Boston Lodge yard on 22 August 2001. *John Morgan, MJS collection*

UPNOR CASTLE: We are now into more modern designs. *Upnor Castle* was a 2ft 6in-gauge 180bhp loco built for the Chattenden & Upnor Railway in 1954 by F. C. Hibberd & Co Ltd, a British firm founded in 1927. It subsequently found itself on the Welshpool & Llanfair Railway, and was bought by the FR in 1968 and converted to the railway's 1ft 11½in gauge. It is seen here standing in Boston Lodge yard on 29 July 1991. It was sold to the WHR Construction Company in 1996, but has now effectively returned to FR operational stock, after a decade's hard work building the new line. *MJS*

MOEL HEBOG: Though looking decidedly more ancient, this loco is in fact one year younger than *Upnor Castle*! New from Hunslet in 1955, it was initially supplied to the National Coal Board as a flameproof mines locomotive. Since arriving on the FR in 1969 it has acquired a cab and footplate and, following work on the 'deviation', is now predominantly used on permanent way duties. It is seen here in Minffordd yard on 27 March 1983. *John Morgan, MJS collection*

CONWAY CASTLE: Initially built in 1958 by F. C. Hibberd for the Admiralty, and similar to *Upnor Castle*, it was purchased by the FR in 1981 and upgraded for main-line passenger work. It is now allocated to Dinas shed on the recently restored Welsh Highland Railway. It is graced with bilingual names, the Welsh version being *Castell Conwy*. On 15 June 1991 it is about to leave Harbour station with an FR passenger duty. *John Morgan, MJS collection*

CRICCIETH CASTLE: Another loco with bilingual names, *Criccieth* was built in-house, in 1995, from parts supplied by Baguley-Drewry, and included braking equipment from a BR Class 08 shunter. A relatively small 0-6-0DM locomotive, it is deceptively powerful, having been upgraded with a Caterpillar engine. When rebuilt it was also equipped for 'push-pull' working, a facility no longer required by the FR, but it is still to be found at the head of passenger trains. It is seen here in Boston Lodge yard on 4 August 2003. *John Morgan, MJS collection*

HARLECH CASTLE: Baguley-Drewry was also involved with this loco, but this time as builder. Intended for service in Mozambique, the order was subsequently cancelled and the FR stepped in and bought it in 1988. Again bilingually named, it is used wholly by the PW/CE Department and is accordingly painted in their yellow and grey livery; it also lacks vacuum brake equipment, so cannot be 'stolen' by the operating railway! Much of its time is spent in Minffordd yard, as here on 22 June 1996. *John Morgan, MJS collection*

VALE OF FFESTINIOG: We have previously seen this loco 'in action' on page 104. Built in South Africa by C. H. Funkey & Co Ltd in 1967 for the Eastern Province Cement Co in Port Elizabeth, it came to the FR, with its 'sister' loco now on the Welsh Highland Railway, in 1996. Extensively rebuilt and now unrecognisable from its original design, it provides options to the railway in terms of both power and fuel, as well as providing a 'turn the key' rescue loco capable of recovering any FR passenger train. This is another view of it at Blaenau Ffestiniog, in National Power colours, on 18 April 1998. *MJS*

As inherited by the railway, the telegraph route across the Cob was by way of standard telegraph poles with wires. Faced with the vagaries of wind and weather on this mile-long stretch of exposed real estate, among other considerations, the railway decided to improve matters. To also assist the Gwynedd River Board, which wished to strengthen the seaward side of the embankment, the S&T Department removed the poles and wires. In this view from early July 1963, the work is in hand, with the new multi-core cable progressively being laid on the outside base of the wave wall. Being before the high season, before the school holidays, the thinner train service of the day gives opportunities for work. *Norman Pearce, Howard Wilson collection*

A superb demonstration of how approaches to volunteer work have changed over the years. On an unidentified date in the mid-1970s, members of the Midlands Group are engaged in installing a line of former standard-gauge sleepers, which had been among various materials recovered by the FR from Old Dalby in Leicestershire, between the running line and the public footpath along the Cob, to retain the railway's ballast and prevent it being trodden down by walkers using the path. Note the complete absence of hi-vis vests, and that single hand tools are being wielded by incredibly smartly dressed individuals!

The second scene is from November 1985, and by now the advice that more workaday gear was recommended has been heeded. At the north end of Tan y Bwlch station a busy group of volunteers are hard at work digging a ditch in preparation for the installation of cables for the electric signalling. *Both Tony Baker*

Shotcreting duties in 1978: the concrete was transferred from a road vehicle into this 'torpedo' car, then a retardant was mixed with it to keep it flowable, and an accelerator combined at the spray head to make it stick. Bunny Lewis is on top of it. Andy Putnam built the FR concrete unit from a truck mixer mounted on an Isle of Man wagon frame, and it was used on many mass concrete jobs. *Tony Baker*

The Midlands Group is in action again, in February 1977, loading ballast into a wagon before proceeding to lay it between the then terminus at Llyn Ystradau and Tanygrisiau, in preparation for the reopening to the latter the following year. This is definitely a job calling for a hot bath or shower at the end of the day! The shark-tooth-painted RAF 'waggon' (so spelled in the 1832 Act) was painted in haste and in the dark by Fred Howes to indicate that the end door would not lift out – to get one of these in a cutting where the side doors would not drop made one angry, hence the paint job – they were known as 'Sharks'! (BR also had ballast wagons called 'Sharks'.) *Tony Baker*

After 1980, the work to ensure the return of the railway to Blaenau Ffestiniog was hotting up, with rails snaking their way from the terminus at Tanygrisiau. On a beautifully sunny day in 1981, Andy Putnam supervises the Midland Group at Glan y Pwll in ballasting during the 'Building Back to Blaenau' phase. In the background can be seen the footbridge to the now closed school, and two of the volunteers, Dave Payling and Ian Touloose. Both locos are 20hp Simplexes (Simplices?), with *Diane* at the rear and *The Colonel* at the front. *Tony Baker*

Largely unnoticed by the general public as they go about the railway, other than using them for their benefit, the signs at various locations have both to be created by the railway, then maintained/renewed at intervals. Much of the signage is custom-made in the Gweithdy workshop adjacent to Minffordd station. A steady hand and concentration are needed, as can be seen from this view of Tammy Stretton putting the finishing touches to the logo of the iconic Double-Fairlie, just before she breaks for lunch on 15 March 2009. *Judi Stretton*

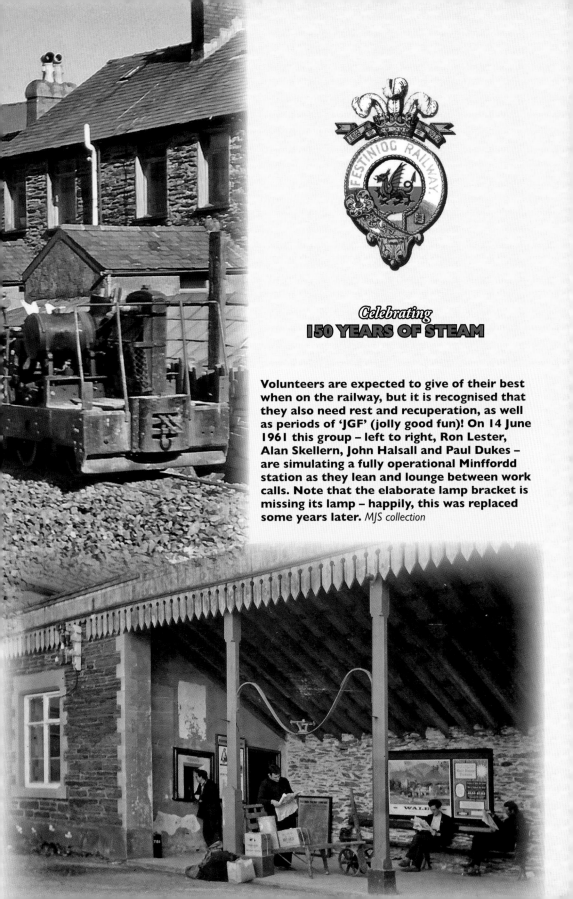

Celebrating
150 YEARS OF STEAM

Volunteers are expected to give of their best when on the railway, but it is recognised that they also need rest and recuperation, as well as periods of 'JGF' (jolly good fun)! On 14 June 1961 this group – left to right, Ron Lester, Alan Skellern, John Halsall and Paul Dukes – are simulating a fully operational Minffordd station as they lean and lounge between work calls. Note that the elaborate lamp bracket is missing its lamp – happily, this was replaced some years later. *MJS collection*

And so as we come to the end we can catch a train to take us back to our departure point. With the driver studiously looking ahead, *Earl of Merioneth* rounds the curve into Tanygrisiau station on Monday 11 June 2012 with the 1510 Blaenau Ffestiniog-Porthmadog service, in driving rain. The left-hand track will take us back to Porthmadog, whereas the right-hand one can transport us to pastures new! *MJS*